Letters to Garrett

Robert E. Quinn, Garrett T. Quinn

Letters to Garrett

Stories of Change, Power, and Possibility

JOSSEY-BASS
A Wiley Company
www.josseybass.com

Published by

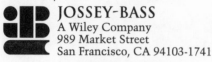 **JOSSEY-BASS**
A Wiley Company
989 Market Street
San Francisco, CA 94103-1741

www.josseybass.com

Credits appear on page 236.

Library of Congress Cataloging-in-Publication Data H2C

Quinn, Robert E.
    Letters to Garrett : stories of change, power, and possibility
/ Robert E. Quinn, Garrett T. Quinn.
        p. cm. — (The Jossey-Bass business & management series)
        ISBN 0-7879-6115-9 (alk. paper)
        1. Teenage boys—Conduct of life. 2. Young men—Conduct of life.
I. Quinn, Garrett T. II. Title. III. Series.
    BJ1671 .Q85 2002
    158—dc21   2001008203

FIRST EDITION

HB Printing   10 9 8 7 6 5 4 3 2 1

The Jossey-Bass
Business & Management Series

Contents

To Delsa Quinn,
a woman we both love intensely

Preface

Robert's Preface

I have a son who recently graduated from high school. In high school he had life all figured out. He was a big man on campus. Suddenly he was leaving the world in which he so successfully operated. The transition proved most difficult. He spent much of his freshman year in college wrestling with depression. He seemed to feel negatively about everyone, including me. He was having a hard time getting to classes or doing much of anything. He was caught in a vicious circle in which his world just kept getting darker.

I agonized, prayed, and struggled to find some way to help. I wanted to fix things, to solve the problem. Gradually I came to an important realization. The real problem was that I was seeing my son as a problem, something to be fixed. The painful truth was that he was not a problem in need of fixing. He was a human being in need of love. He was just like every other human being in a period of transition. As he tried to figure out who he was and where he was going, his primary need was for love and support.

The dreadful truth is that I was failing and I was the one who needed to change. I needed to be more connected, more loving and supportive to a son who seemed to be pushing me away. This was not an easy challenge. I had to do something outside the box. I needed some structure that would ensure regular communication. I had no idea what that structure might look like.

As I continued to wrestle, I felt a sense of inspiration and gradually came to a strategy. I invited my son to coauthor a book with me. We would do this by exchanging letters. I hoped he would find the proposal attractive. He did. At a time when he was unwilling to commit to much of anything, including going to his classes, he committed to joining me in writing. That was promising.

Over the course of a year, the book did become a structure or a discipline in the creation of relationship. I searched my entire base of experience. I explored my own dark times. I shared my most effective tools for self-leadership. His first letters were very short and concise. Then they got a little longer. As he commented on my letters, he shared his own feelings and experiences. We began to communicate about things we could not talk about earlier. Those conversations became increasingly enriched. Last week, in getting the manuscript ready, we had a spontaneous discussion about one of the concepts in the book. At a certain point I shared some deeply held personal feelings, and a few tears flowed. He listened with empathy, and the result was loving communion. A couple of nights later, the boy who last year did not want me near him laid his head on my knee while we sat in the living room and talked to friends. These may seem like small things, but I consider them significant markers in the journey we have made together.

He is still doing those nineteen-year-old things that parents agonize over. Yet I no longer react to them the way I once did. They do not seem to matter so much. Today I see my son with more loving eyes. I see awesome potential. I more fully confirm his right to make decisions and bumble his way forward in life, just as I have bumbled my way forward. There is nothing there to fix, but there is someone there to love. There always was.

This book is the story of an unfolding relationship, as well as a discussion of how to live more effectively and how to change so as to live with increased power and possibility. The book has many audiences. The book is for people like my son, those who are facing a first great transition. It is for those trying to help a loved one through a transition. It is for people like me, adults in the professional world who want to contribute but find that life is not such an easy puzzle. In other words, this book is written for anyone who needs a little help in facing the demons that seek to prevent human progress. My son needed it. In trying to provide it, I found out I needed it. You may also need it. As you read these pages, it is my hope that they bring you to a life of more productive change and greater power and possibility.

February 2002   ROBERT E. QUINN
Ann Arbor, Michigan

Garrett's Preface

I used to like roller coasters. I've ridden some of the biggest. But none of them provided a ride like the one I've been on in the past three years. I have been to the greatest of heights and the worst of depths. In the past year, as I approached those depths, I felt lost. I had no constant in my life, save the unconditional love and prayers of those closest to me. For all I know, these people saved my life.

Things always came relatively easy for me. Growing up, I did well in school. I had a great family life. I played a number of different sports and was solid in all of them. I had everything going for me.

In high school I did not work much but kept a B average.
I had lots of friends and a great girlfriend, and I was able to play
basketball.

In my junior year we had a great basketball team. I was the
starting shooting guard. We had a great regular season and then
won the Michigan state championship. It was something that no
other team from my school had ever done. The feeling of success
was exhilarating.

In my senior year we ended the regular season 18–2. That
was the best regular season record in the history of the school. We
felt ready to make another run at the state title. I became deeply
determined and completely focused on winning the tournament.

We won the first five games of the tournament and again
earned a berth in the state quarterfinals. I was sure that we would
win it all. But it wasn't meant to be. In that quarterfinal game we
managed to keep the score close until the last moments, but the
other team broke away at the end, and we lost.

We had done everything we were supposed to do. I couldn't
understand what had happened. For the next few weeks I was in a
disoriented state. I rarely spoke to anyone, and when I did, it was
always one or two words. I was really struggling to cope with the
loss. I had poured my heart and soul into that year, that team, and
that game. Yet I had failed. It was a terrible feeling.

I felt like a loser, and I needed a way to get away from the
pain. I started drinking. I went to class less, partied more, and
gambled a lot. I just focused on having a good time with all of my
friends before we all went away to college. I pushed my problems
away and pretended that everything was fine.

When I got to college, I figured things would get better.
I was wrong. I had little in common with my roommates. The
apartment was always a mess. As the year went on I dreaded my

living situation more and more. I also struggled with my classes. I only had eleven credit hours, but I rarely went to class and never studied.

I started to gamble more seriously, and soon I was gambling away all of my money. The more I lost, the more desperate I got. Eventually I lost it all. I had squandered $3,000.

After that, I just stopped functioning. I went to bed by ten o'clock every night and I wouldn't get up until two the next afternoon. I figured the less time I was awake the better. I began to think about death. It didn't seem all that bad to me. Although I never acted on those thoughts, I did have them. I realized I could never do that. It would cause too much pain for my mom.

This was around the time that my dad asked me to help write this book. I didn't really know what to think at first. I didn't really want to do it. I figured it was just some way for him to try and build our relationship. At the time I didn't want to build any relationships, especially not one with my dad. I felt angry with him. I am not sure why, but I did.

For some reason, I said yes to the book project. I found that the letters were interesting and found myself using some of the ideas to help myself feel a little better about life.

But there were no easy answers. I wanted a cure, but there wasn't one. I felt useless. I didn't care about anything. Toward the end of the year I started drinking again, nearly every night.

Then I had a big test.

One Saturday night I stopped by to say hello to some friends. I didn't plan to stay out. But the people I was with started drinking and invited me to join them. Since I didn't have anything to do the next day, I told myself it was OK. I got pretty drunk. Then a group of us got together and started smoking pot. We smoked a lot, and I was really messed up.

All I remember after that was taking a step back and trying to get away from the people I was with. I was really paranoid and thought they were trying to kill me. It turned out that they nearly did.

I don't know exactly what happened after that, but this is what I've extracted from a number of different accounts. I had passed out and was pretty much gone. I wouldn't respond to anybody. At that point I stopped breathing normally. I wasn't getting enough oxygen to my brain. Luckily, one kid thought I needed to go to the hospital. None of the others wanted to take me. The kid who was helping eventually got some other guys to help get me into his car. Then he drove me to the hospital. He saved my life.

When I woke up, my mom and dad were standing over me. I was strapped down because I had been convulsing. My legs and arms were completely tied down. When I was semiconscious, I remember spitting at the doctor. I thought he was trying to kill me.

I had needles in both of my arms and my chest. There were tubes in my nose, and I was catheterized. I remember telling my mom that she was the reason I was alive. Somewhere in my mind I felt like she had kept me from dying. I knew that I couldn't leave her. I knew that she wouldn't be able to handle it if I died. I had already caused her so much pain. I think God decided that it wasn't my time.

That night was a turning point. The next day I decided that I was going to make the terrible experience positive by learning and changing. I would improve my life.

That brings me to now. I'm taking the year off from school. I'm working full time. I'm trying to get some discipline back into my life before I go back to school. I'm an assistant varsity basketball coach at the high school. I'm excited about that.

But the most important thing is that I'm happy. I've begun to love all of the little things life has to offer. I keep a positive attitude most of the time, and I rarely feel depressed. I'm no longer on my prescribed medication, and I am happy to be alive. I wasn't always. I went through some remarkably dark times. I often think no one else could understand what that was like. But I know that there are millions of people out there going through similar trials.

There were periods when I didn't care whether I lived or died. The thing that kept me from seriously considering suicide was relationships. I knew that there were people who cared for and loved me. I could never hurt them. The people I worry about are those who don't have a support system like mine.

My recent experiences have been difficult, far and away the worst time of my life. But here is the strange thing: I wouldn't trade my experience. I learned so many things about life and about myself. I learned about love and its power. Though I did not make it easy for people to love me, they loved me anyway. They extended themselves. Now I want to love everybody that same way. That is why I have told this story. Writing it has not been easy. It has taken more courage than I knew I had. But writing it will be worth it all if it helps someone else keep going. That is my hope— that this book and my story will help someone choose to change, to learn, to grow, and to live a more meaningful life.

February 2002   GARRETT T. QUINN
Ann Arbor, Michigan

Letters to Garrett

Introduction: Seek to Make a Difference

Dear Garrett,

Last month I was invited to give a guest lecture for an under-graduate class of juniors and seniors. It was a course on change. I decided not to prepare a presentation. I wanted to make a difference by attending to their most central needs. But I seldom have contact with undergraduates, so I was not sure what those needs might be. When I got there, I asked them to answer two questions for me. My first question was "Now that you have spent almost a semester studying change, what are you sure about?" My second question was "What are you not sure about—that is, what are you struggling with that you think is a really important issue?"

I had them read their answers to question one. They were sure about all kinds of things. They talked about the complexity and unpredictability of the change process. They recited the various conceptual schemes that they had studied during the semester.

We then turned to my second question—what they were not sure about and what issues they were struggling with that they felt were really important. I made a list of the answers they gave. Some of them wanted to know how to find an organization that would value them and let them actually try to make changes. Some wanted to know how to keep from getting neutralized by the organization. A few asked, "How do I get anything done in an organization when I know there will be resistance to anything I propose that is significant and valuable?" There were people who wanted to know how to make changes in their families. The list went on. Finally, an especially petite woman who was sitting in the front row said, "I am about to graduate from the University of Michigan, yet I look like I am twelve years old. How am I going to get anyone, anywhere, to listen to what I have to say?"

Everyone laughed, a very friendly kind of laughter. In her own way she was articulating what everyone was asking: How do I establish credibility? How do I get heard? How do I exert influence? Is it possible for me to have impact, to make a difference? How do I lead change?

I told the students that I would not answer their specific questions but would speak to the key issues that I heard them expressing in all their questions: How can I be a change agent, to have an impact, to make a meaningful difference in the world?

That question is really important. I think it is important to every young person. Yet our concerns about how to make a difference never go away, regardless of our age or other circumstances. These are concerns of everyone.

I can remember asking myself this same question when I was a college student. It was very important to me. It still is. In fact, my life was and is pretty much structured around this question. Let me explain.

When I was twenty-one, I returned to school after a two-year experience as a missionary. I had just completed an amazing adventure focused on helping other people change their lives.

To do that work required enormous personal discipline. As I struggled to exercise such discipline I began to grow. I also began to connect to people in new ways. I began to contribute. People's lives were altered. These people made decisions and lived better lives because of the relationship we built. Those encounters brought more meaning into my life than anything I had ever experienced before.

At the end of my mission, I returned to college. I went to the bookstore and bought introductory textbooks in a number of the usual disciplines. After a week or so of classes, I began to notice how tired I felt. I was sleeping late every day. I was going back to my room to take afternoon naps. I was going to bed early. I was not ill. I just felt very tired. The only thing that seemed to interest me was playing basketball. I spent a lot of time in pickup games at the gym. And sleeping.

Several months went by. Then one day as I was walking to my room at my dorm, I mentioned to a friend how very tired I was feeling. He looked at me in disgust. "You aren't tired," he said, "you're depressed." He walked away, and I stood there in shock. His words hit me like lightning. He was right. It was undeniable. I was depressed. I was not sure why, but I was depressed.

I started to analyze myself. What was I feeling? The first thing I noted was that I hated my classes. I had some good teachers and some bad ones, but the quality of teaching did not seem to matter. Those introductory books and the class content just seemed so irrelevant. Why would anyone care about any of that stuff?

I began to ask myself what I wanted to do with my life. I had no idea. I asked myself what I wanted to major in. I had no idea. I was lost. I had no sense of direction, no sense of growth. Given my missionary experience, I began to pray about a major. This proved futile. I didn't get anything even approaching an answer or an insight.

My feelings about lacking any purpose or meaning started to drive me crazy. Finally I decided to fast and pray. I fasted twice. Still, no answers came. I decided to try one more time. The day of that last fast, I was walking home from class asking myself what I should major in. Suddenly I had one of the most memorable spiritual experiences of my life. I received a direct answer. The answer came in the form of a new question: "Up to now, what is the most significant thing you have ever done?"

That question came out of the blue. But it was like drawing the "Get Out of Jail Free" card in the game Monopoly. I had an immediate response. The most significant thing I had ever done was discipline myself to grow and form relationships with people in such a way that their lives and mine were elevated in significant and lasting ways. The answer to my prayer was clear: "Major in change."

It was a thrilling answer except for one little problem. The university didn't offer a major in change. How do you take courses in something that doesn't even exist?

For the first time in my life I became assertive about education. Like most people in the world, I guess I had always looked on education as something other people did to me. It was imposed on me. Formal education was an institution that one put up with in order to have a social life. I remember feeling that for the most part it was a mediocre institution that produced mediocre results.

I began asking myself how I could get what I wanted from the university. I was committed to majoring in change, but to do that I had to become a guerrilla fighter. I had to dig information out of courses and attend public lectures about change. I soon found out that the courses were scattered. So I figured out that I could pick one of their existing majors and slant it toward the study of change. This was no easy task, and I lost a lot of battles. But as I pursued this plan, my depression disappeared. I was being less externally directed—acted on—by the educational institution. I was taking greater charge of creating myself by becoming more internally directed, more self-initiating.

I began to read books that offered answers to the questions I found myself asking. I began to read books that offered answers to the questions I found myself asking. I began to approach professors with my own questions. They were not smart-aleck questions but questions driven by my hunger to know. To my surprise, the professors were surprised. Most of them welcomed my questions. They were not used to students with a passion to know. I got to know some of my professors on a more equal basis. Prior to the changes I'd made, that had seemed unthinkable. The chasm I'd once felt between teachers and students was suddenly gone.

I began to notice that not all professors were created equal. And so I made a new rule: I would never again take a course. I would only take professors! I would only spend my time in classrooms with great teachers. The lesson I'd pass on to you is to never sign up for a course in which the teacher does not care or is only a normal teacher. To do so is a grievous mistake.

Another thing I learned is that great teaching comes in many packages and styles. Some of my best teachers were dynamic, loving people. Some were very low key but filled with brilliant wisdom. Some were not at all student-friendly but were passionate about the subject they taught. Learning can unfold in many ways. Seek out teachers with a reputation for greatness. Demand excellence in teaching. Hold the university to high standards.

I have never regretted my decision to try to take only great teachers. I must warn you, though, that if you choose this path, it will require even more effort on your part. To get a quality education, you have to become an assertive student, a guerrilla fighter. We all tend to be trained to be passive consumers of education. But if you want to make a difference and to make an impact in your life, you have to realize that the responsibility for getting a quality education falls on your shoulders.

This kind of talk makes my colleagues very uncomfortable. One pointed out that there is only a limited supply of good teachers and so not everyone can follow my advice. My response is that most people will not follow my advice. Everyone wants to take great teachers, but most students are not willing to make a concerted effort. Most will not go the extra mile. I expect no revolutionary demand on the university.

Well, as you probably know, I graduated in sociology, but I was and continue to be a student of change. I soon discovered that a new field was being born, called "organizational development." It was about the practice of change. As I pursued a Ph.D., I continued to focus on the question of how to bring change into the world. My guerrilla tactics with the institution continued, but in the end I received what I had set out to get—an education focused on change. Since that time I have focused my teaching, consulting practice, research, and writing on change. I have focused my life on the questions asked last month by the students in that undergraduate class.

Hearing young men and women in that class ask those questions made me think about you. I suspect that as you travel through your freshman year, you will be asking questions such as "What should I do with my life?" "How do I establish credibility?" "How do I get heard?" "How do I exert influence?" "Is it possible for me to have impact and make a difference?" "How can I emerge as a leader or change agent?" "How can I learn to make a meaningful difference in the world?"

I think I have some of the answers to those questions. They have to do with something I call "being change." I would like to pass along to you what I've discovered about the notion of being change and how *being change is leading change.* Along the way, I will try to hold myself to the same standards of excellence that I have suggested you demand from your teachers in the classroom.

Love,

Dad

Focus on Being Change

Dear Garrett,

Thank you for your reply. It is great to hear what is on your mind. I love you with all my heart and want you to know that no matter what you do or do not do, in my eyes you already are, and always will be, a very bright star. Thinking about you and your potential always warms my heart. By the way, happy birthday!

In your response to the last letter you paint a dark picture. I thought the following paragraph was particularly central:

> *I thought the first letter was very interesting. I can relate to a lot of the things you talk about. The notion of being disconnected from what goes on in classes, for example. I feel very disconnected, and school isn't that interesting to me. I sleep a lot, and some people might say that I'm depressed. I'm not sure about that, though. I have this problem with beating myself up. I never did it before. But lately I've been doing it a lot. I just feel like I'm a waste. In your letter you talked about when you were depressed and how you slept all the time and did not want to do anything. That is how it is for me. I feel little motivation to do things. I am not growing. I feel like I haven't done much with my God-given abilities. It's sad to me. But I don't have much desire to do anything about it. So maybe I am depressed. If I am, I don't think it's very severe.*

I'm sorry you are having such a hard time. I suspect that you feel pretty unique. Yet I also know that everyone has some variation of this same experience. There are armies of college-age people who feel just as you do. But it is not just college-age people. It is everyone. Even at my age, I frequently get to a point when I have some of the same feelings you describe. When I have them, I feel stuck. I get trapped in some kind of vicious cycle and can see no way out. I just keep doing things that seem to get me more stuck. And pretty soon it all seems so hopeless.

The good news is that I can offer some ideas about getting out of the prison you are in. In the last letter I said that we are all concerned about the capacity to have influence and impact. I also brought up the subject of "being change." I have three stories I'd like to share with you that illustrate what I mean about being change. One of these stories is about your sister, one is about you, and one is about a woman in a professional organization. They all illustrate a principle I think you might find valuable.

The first story is about your oldest sister. One day your mom and I received a phone call from her. Shauri was distraught. She had been getting very serious about a young man, Matt, with whom she had invested a great deal emotionally. He had just told her he was going to break off their relationship, and now there was only pain. She felt rejected and hurt. She was churning with negative feelings. She announced that she was coming home to recover. When the phone conversation ended, your mom indicated that I should fulfill my fatherly responsibilities and pick up Shauri at the airport.

Shauri climbed into the car and immediately started talking about her unfortunate situation. She was flooded with negative emotions, and we talked at length about the agony of relationships and attraction. Yet nothing seemed to ease her pain. She was in a deep emotional hole, and as she agonized, the hole seemed only to get deeper and darker. Finally I asked her, "Are you problem-solving or purpose-finding?" The strange question jolted her, and she looked at me quizzically.

I suggested that most people tend to live their lives in a reactive mode. They are always trying to solve their problems.

Their problems are a source of pain, and they want the pain to go away. Their problems ebb and flow in intensity but tend not to go away. People are then sad or happy, depending on where they are in the ebb and flow. This is very common. It is how normal people live—in a reactive stance.

Shauri asked what the alternative was. I suggested that instead of being reactors, we can be actors, initiators, or creators. When we initiate, we tend to eventually create value, and we tend to feel good about ourselves. If we continually clarify our most noble purposes, they become a magnet. We are drawn toward them. No matter what emotions we feel, we begin to pursue our purpose. When we do begin to pursue our purpose, our negative emotions tend to disappear. We experience victory over the reactive self, and we feel good about who we are. We feel better because we literally begin to have a more valuable self. We are empowered, and we become empowering to others.

Shauri was not buying it. She ignored me and then spent another fifteen minutes complaining about how unfair life could be. She paused for a breath, and I again asked her if she was problem-solving or purpose-finding. She ignored my question and continued venting. We repeated this pattern four times. The last time I asked, she stopped talking and just looked at me. I could tell a big challenge was coming. To put an end to my insensitive questioning, she asked, "How would I ever use purpose-finding in this situation?"

"You can use it in any situation," I replied.

She asked, "How do *you* do it?"

I said, "Whenever I am feeling lost or filled with negative emotions, I get out my life statement and rewrite it."

We were turning into the driveway. "What is a life statement?" she asked.

I explained that it is a short document in which I try to capture the essence of who I am and what my purpose is in life.

"You have an actual document that does that?" She seemed truly surprised.

Something had changed. She was expressing genuine curiosity. She had, for a moment, changed her focus from her bad fortune, and she wanted to know more about my strange claims. This was a window. I saw that there was a possibility for joining with her at a more meaningful level. She was momentarily open. If we could stay on this track, our souls might begin to touch more deeply. We might more openly exchange ideas and feelings. New images might emerge, and a transformation might take place. Here was a chance for meaningful contact and entrance to the reality of profound possibility. That is what happened.

I said, "Let me show you my life statement."

She followed me into my study. I reached into a file, pulled out a sheet of paper, and handed it to her. It is the same sheet of paper that I've enclosed to you in this letter. (*Note:* It is reprinted in the Appendix at the back of this book. You might want to go there and read it at this time.)

Shauri read the document carefully and then looked up. She was fascinated. She asked, "When you feel bad, you read this and it makes you feel better?"

"No, when I feel really bad, I take my life statement out, read it carefully, and try to rewrite any part of it that I feel needs revision. Or I add something that was not there before. The document is always evolving. When I finish rewriting it, I feel clearer about who I am. By knowing what I value most, I become stable. To make change, I have to become stable at one level so that I can change at some other level. If my values are clear and stable, I can confront the issues that previously made me feel confused and fearful. My "being state" changes. I become more proactive in my stance. I have the energy to move forward no matter how negative my emotions. In fact, my negative emotions tend to disappear before I even start to act. Just clarifying who I am and what I want to create seems to energize me. Even the thought of movement becomes purifying."

I paused for a moment as Shauri took in my words. Then I continued: "There is another reason for rewriting. People think that values are permanent, like cement. Clear values can stabilize us, yet they are living systems and need to be allowed to evolve. Each time we face a new situation and reinterpret our values, they change just a little bit. Rewriting a statement like this one allows us to integrate what we have learned and how we have developed into our values. Hence our values also evolve with us. We cocreate each other."

Shauri told me it was difficult to understand some of the words in my life statement. I agreed that this was true because the document is not written for anyone but me. I have written it over and over, and it has become more and more personalized. It reflects my private, innermost language. I have invented some of that language for me. I told her I have executives in my classes write their own, and they always begin with very simple life statements. She asked how she might apply her own life statement in her situation. I suggested that instead of spending the weekend feeling bad about what happened and working through all her reactions to the event, she might instead spend the time writing her own life statement. She would thus move from being a reactor to becoming an actor. I reflected that many people spend their lives being acted on and that I believe we are meant to create, not just to react.

Shauri indicated she would start writing her own life statement, and she did. By the end of the weekend, she was ready to return home. A few days later she sent me a copy of an amazing letter. She has given me permission to share it with you. I would like to present it in parts and make a few observations on each part.

Shauri had written this letter to your brother and sister. She began it by describing her painful experience and her decision to fly home. This is what she said:

Dad picked me up from the airport, and on the way home he started to ask me questions about what and how I was feeling about the situation with Matt. At first the focus was just on the pain I was feeling and self-pity as I wondered what was wrong with me and if I would ever find anyone to love. I was just going over and over the problem. Dad turned the conversation from "solving my problem" to "finding my purpose." My gut reaction initially was to bring it back to the problem. I wanted to wallow in the pain of the problem. I thought I was looking for a solution, but it wasn't until I allowed the conversation to really flow into my purpose that I found the solution.

Negative emotions pull us into the reactive mode. They drain us of energy and lead us to quit. We are dammed—and damned—by our negative emotions; we cease to move, initiate, or create and therefore cease to grow. When I talked about finding purpose, as Shauri points out, she wanted to return to the pain. In doing so, she duped herself into believing that she was trying to solve her problem. But in truth this prevented her from acting. When she at last moved into finding her purpose, her entire outlook changed.

As I thought about this, the realization came to me that I should start looking to purify my life right now. This tied into Dad's ideas of focusing on purpose rather than problems. In working to purify my life, I would be focusing on service and things of higher purpose rather than on my day-to-day problems. Doing this would take care of the problem.

After describing these insights, Shauri's letter made a surprising turn. She shared an e-mail message she had recently sent to Matt. It turns out he had contacted her and indicated he missed hearing from her. In her response to him she wrote the following:

WELL, the last thing I want you to go through is e-mail withdrawal. That can be painful for anyone. And it is so easily remedied!

I was really sad after our talk—more than I thought I would be. I still can't totally pinpoint why. I think a lot of it was because even though I was never 100 percent sure of whether we were right, I still put more into our relationship than I ever have with anyone else. I opened myself up to hurt, and I don't usually do that. It was a good growing time for me, though. I also think rejection hurts regardless of how you feel for someone or why they do it, so I probably felt bad that you didn't LOVE me. Finally I think it hurt because I spent a good bulk of my time with you since May and I felt I wasn't just losing a potential relationship but also a good friend. Separation is not my strong point.

So that is my analysis of my pain. You didn't realize you were opening up the door for all of this information by e-mailing, did you?

Anyway, this weekend was so good for me. I had the best talk with my dad. He picked me up at the airport, and we started talking about how and why I felt sad about you, and it moved into his recent letter about problem-solving versus purpose-finding. We started talking about what I needed to do to purify myself. He suggested that I needed a vision. He said that if I clarified my purpose, all the peripheral problems that seemed big (like my talk with you) would disappear and take care of themselves. I was so motivated by this.

I'm going to send you a copy of the letter my dad wrote about this. The focus on purpose is something that I think you might find helpful in your life right now. My dad and I also talked about making conversations more meaningful and sharing spiritual intimacies with people. I won't go into that right now, but it was a great topic for me too. I was just excited to make some changes and find a vision. The reason I'm sharing all of this with you is that I feel that the process of deciding how we felt about each other actually deepened our relationship. I learned to communicate more effectively because of you and to open myself up and share all kinds of feelings, so the outcome is that I feel I can still share anything with you. I hope you feel the same about me. I think we've established a great friendship, and I hope you feel the same. I think we may have tried to force feelings a little that weren't there—maybe timing was off, maybe it just isn't right now or ever, but I definitely want to keep our friendship. I hope you feel that you can tell me anything and that I will be here for you no matter what, because I will. I appreciate your honesty with me about your feelings. I think what you felt is right. I hope you know I love you!

Shauri

Shauri told me that she had decided to share her e-mail message with her roommates, and they all had the same strong reaction. They argued that the message was too honest! They could never imagine opening themselves up like that to someone who had just rejected them. I suspect that previously Shauri might have agreed with them. Yet something had changed. She was suddenly less normal than before. What Shauri wrote to me next is of great consequence.

*The funny thing is I felt a huge sense of peace about it all.
It was liberating. . . . I was no longer worried about Matt's
response or reaction to me or to what I told him. I chose to
act rather than react. Because I did, it freed me and
empowered me. By giving up control in this situation, I
gained control of the situation. I wasn't worried about Matt's
response. I had been completely honest with him, and
strangely, it gave me confidence. My purpose is to purify
myself and serve others. Since I began working toward
purpose, I have been set free from my problems, and they are
resolving themselves. I feel filled with light, and I know that
as I continue in my purpose, my light will grow brighter and
brighter and I will lose myself in it.*

Shauri's experience illustrates many important points. First,
it is normal to be reactive and to have negative emotions. We are
all pulled in this direction. Though most of us would claim that
we hate the negative emotions we are feeling, we do not behave as
if we do. We in fact often choose to stay in our negative state. We
seem to become addicted to the process of wallowing in "the
problem." It is natural and, in a strange way, comfortable to be in
such pain. At such times, this victim role is our path of least
resistance, and we willingly take it—perhaps because it is a role we
know how to play.

Second, our being state can be controlled. We do not have
to stay in the victim role. We can choose our own response. We do
this by leaving the "external world," where the problem seems to
be located. We go inside ourselves, not to the problem but to our
purpose. When we go inside to clarify our purpose, our perception
is altered dramatically. The original problem does not necessarily
go away, but it becomes much less relevant. We outgrow the problem. It becomes much less important than it was.

Third, our being state changes the world. As soon as Shauri started to clarify her purpose, she felt a sense of progress. Her negative emotions turned positive. She started to feel faith, hope, strength, confidence, and love. The new positive emotions empowered her and made her empowering. She became inner-directed and other-focused. She started to create the relationships in her life. She became a leader. She had made a being change, and now she was leading change. She was a model that others could look to for elevating their own lives.

You may have noticed that since the events I described, there has been a dramatic change in Shauri's life. At the professional level, her career has suddenly taken off. She went from frustration and fear to a bold job change. Her performance on that job has been full of creativity, and she has become a successful young professional. She now loves what she is doing. She presents herself in a much more potent yet peaceful and confident way. Shauri made a change in her being state, and now her external world is dramatically different.

Garrett, I need to tell you that I often get *pushback* from people when I tell them these things. In one form or another, they are saying, "You just do not understand my situation. You do not understand how impossible or grievous it is." And that is exactly what Shauri did at first. She was sure that I did not understand her problem. She perceived my ideas as having no value because her situation was hopeless. You see, my belief is that we can take initiative or lead in any situation. We can lead our impossible boss, our troublesome in-laws, our rebellious children, our resistant peers, or our indifferent employees. We can even lead our roommates! Leading change starts with being change. We can all control who we are. It all begins with asking the right question.

A marvelous book called *The Path of Least Resistance* influenced my thinking on purpose-finding. The author of that book, Robert Fritz, tells us that in any situation we can ask the question, "What result do I want to create?" This is very different from the question we normally ask ourselves, "How do I get what I want?" The first question—*What result do I want to create?*—is about purpose. It is the foundation of the creative life stance. It leads us naturally and powerfully to accountability. It causes us to reframe who we are. It leads us to courageous new behavior. The second question—*How do I get what I want?*—is about process. It is far more limiting than the first question and tends to keep us at our current level of awareness. It keeps us in our comfort zone, which may not be comfortable at all. Consider an example from your own life. You may find it interesting to think about the experience in this new light.

The summer after your team won the state championship, you received that letter inviting you to the Five Star Invitational Basketball Camp. This meant you would spend a week with the hundred best players in the region and that you would be exposed to coaches from the best colleges. When you received the letter, the whole family was really excited. The next morning you walked into the kitchen and announced you were not going. Everyone reacted. I asked you what you were going to do instead. Your response was a teenage classic: "I am going to stay here and chill." You had what seemed like an enticing opportunity. We wanted you to take it. Yet we were not very sensitive to what you might have been feeling. Attending the camp meant going alone to a new place and exposing yourself to high competition. As I put myself in that situation now, I can imagine feelings I might have had.

I suspect I would have been a little fearful of going alone to a place of high competition. Instead of facing that discomfort, I would have asked myself the very normal question, the question we all ask ourselves all the time: "How do I get what I want?" What I probably would have wanted most was to avoid the discomfort of being alone and the risk of the potential embarrassment and failure. I would not have wanted to experience such negative emotions. None of us does. Like you, I probably would have said, "I am just going to stay home and chill."

Now suppose at that time I had asked you, "What result do you want to create in your basketball life?" You might have answered that you wanted to play at a good school. If that had been your answer, and if you had been clear about it, you might have redefined the opportunity. If you were clear and passionate about the potential result you wanted to create, you might have been willing to take the risks involved and thus move forward into the uncomfortable process of engaging the new and highly challenging situation.

The critical point to see now is that what you did was natural. It's what I would have done. We all do it all the time. We are all you. We are all Shauri. We all go through life asking, "How do I get what I want?" and since we yearn to stay on the path of least resistance, we make decisions that keep us there. We create prisons for ourselves and then choose to live in them. We are incarcerated not by steel bars but by our own fears. I have thought about creating a bumper sticker: "THE MOST DANGEROUS PLACE ON EARTH— OUR COMFORT ZONE."

When I say we are all like you, I really mean it. I spend much of my time in universities and in corporations with very intelligent and highly paid people. In all these places, I find what I find elsewhere—people imprisoned by their fears. I believe that success is not guaranteed by college degrees or by holding high positions. All human beings get stuck in their fears and yearn to stay in their comfort zones. All of us slip into the reactive mode. We then suffer and everyone around us suffers. Consider another example.

Recently a woman in a corporation asked to talk to me privately. We went off to an empty office and sat down. She was the director of marketing in the company. She spoke for a few moments, and then tears filled her eyes. She indicated that her predecessor had hired a small army of M.B.A.'s. Since her industry was considered very stodgy and M.B.A.'s normally avoid it, her predecessor's accomplishment in this hiring was considered an impressive victory. He received many accolades.

After this man left, she made an astounding discovery. He had succeeded in hiring the M.B.A.'s by promising them things that no one could possibly deliver. The M.B.A.'s were discovering the lie, and now they were all starting to leave. In fact, just moments earlier she had received a message informing her that yet another M.B.A. had announced he was leaving. She went on to explain that she was now worried that people would see their departures as her failure and not as an error that she had inherited. Yet there was virtually no way to maintain her integrity and keep the M.B.A.'s. It was an impossible problem, and she was certain she was doomed to failure. She went on and on about the difficulty, about how frustrated and beaten she felt.

Finally I asked her what result she wanted to create. She told me she wanted to keep the M.B.A.'s, but she was certain there was no way to do it. I told her I did not believe that this was really the result she wanted to create. She looked puzzled. I asked, "Why are you here? What difference do you want to make in this company?" Her eyes lit up. "Oh, I have a clear mission. I want to change the entire culture of this company. I want to turn it into a customer-centered corporation."

I asked her how she planned to do that, and she described a thoughtful and potentially workable strategy. I asked if she thought the M.B.A.'s were essential to her strategy. She told me they were. I challenged her again.

"It sounds to me like any bright and committed person could successfully carry out the strategic steps you have outlined. What value is added by having an M.B.A.?"

She pondered this for a moment, and her countenance began to change. As she became more positive, she returned to her problem of credibility. "Won't I lose support if people see me as unable to keep the M.B.A.'s?"

"Possibly," I answered. "But is support necessary for you to create the result you want?"

"Yes."

"How can you generate support for your purpose?"

"Well, I could make my purpose clear to everyone. In every conversation I could talk about the objective to change the culture. I could also share the strategy and indicate that one thing we learned is that the M.B.A.'s do not fit our culture, nor are they necessary to our strategy. My people already sense this, and I think other people do as well."

As she spoke, I could see her confidence grow. Our conversation went on for another half hour. When we parted, she looked like a different woman. She was clear on her purpose. She had a strategy. Her fears were gone, and she was ready to take action.

What is the lesson here? I think it is that we are all Shauri, people who experience devastating events. We are all imprisoned by our fears. We are all locked in our comfort zones. We all tend to lean against the stove and declare, "I am just going to stay here and chill." When we do, we remain normal. We are all that woman from marketing. We remain reactive and filled with fears and other negative emotions. Even as we do these things, we deny that we are doing them. We thus begin to get depressed and begin to slowly die inside. The challenge is to stop problem-solving and to start purpose-finding. When we do this, we suddenly discover that we start to have greater influence and impact. We have made a change in our being state. We have moved from the normal condition of being acted on to the extraordinary condition of being an actor, initiator, and creator. We create our own best self.

So school is not very interesting to you. You sleep a lot. You beat yourself up a lot. You feel like you are a waste. You have not done much with the abilities you have been given. You are sad about it. You are not very motivated. You feel like you need to change, but you do not know where to begin. You are particularly unhappy with the relationships in your apartment and feel you need to get out.

I would like to suggest that you first think back and list the times that you felt that you were acting with purpose. In your mind, try to relive those times as vividly as you can. Ask yourself, "When were the times in my life that I know I was acting rather than being acted on?" Write down the behavior patterns you were in at those times. Describe the impacts you were having and the feelings you were experiencing. Doing this will remind you that you have often been a very bright star indeed. With these positive memories operating in your mind, write the first few sentences of your life statement. It may only be a short paragraph or two. You can use mine as a rough template or entirely create your own. There is no right way to do this except to make it express who you are. Make the statement as simple or as complex as you like. One way to do this is to list each category of your present and future life: intellectual, physical, social, family, professional, spiritual, and so on. Then for each category ask yourself, "What result do I want to create in the short run, medium run, and long run?"

There are some other ideas that I'd like to share with you in the future because I think they might help you refine your life statement and elaborate on it. I will be anxious to hear about your reactions to this letter, whether or not you choose to do any of the things I've described, and what you learn from doing them.

I love you.

Dad

Make the Choice to Be Extraordinary

Dear Garrett,

Thanks so much for your last letter. From what you said it is clear that you are struggling to find the motivation to do much of anything. So I am impressed and very grateful that you can discipline yourself to write to me. Despite the discouragement you express, you seem to be churning a bit and coming to some important insights. I was impressed by the following:

> *I see that I'm at an important crossroads in my life right now. I can either continue down this dark path that I am on, or I can try to become more like the person I used to be. I need to make some decisions that I have been putting off. I need to do some purpose-finding. It is just so hard to get started with any kind of positive action. Another thing that you might find interesting is that I believe I'm starting to regain my love for people. In the past eight months of my life, I haven't had a very positive outlook on anything, especially not where other people are concerned. I have been extremely judgmental and unfair toward the people around me. I used to love people for who they are, and now I hate them for no reason at all. It's something that I want to change.*

I find it encouraging that you can so clearly see the difference between the present and the past and that you want to get closer to the person you used to be. It is striking to hear you talk about difficulty with people when maintaining positive relationships has always been such a strong characteristic of yours. I think that you are right that purpose-finding might be helpful. I want to pass the following statement on to you because I feel it does a good job of explaining why it is so important to focus on purpose-finding rather than problem-solving. It is a quote from the writings of a man I have mentioned in an earlier letter, Robert Fritz (1989).

> *But upon close examination, problems are most often irrelevant. As a way of life, not much can come out of problem solving. After years of dedicated work on the subject, psychologist Carl Jung made this astute observation: All the greatest and most important problems of life are fundamentally insoluble. They can never be solved, but only outgrown. This "out-growth" proved on further investigation to require a new level of consciousness. Some higher or wider interest appeared on the patient's horizon, and through this broadening of his or her outlook the insoluble problem lost its urgency. It was not solved logically in its own terms but faded when confronted with a new and stronger life urge.*

What strikes me as important here is that when we clarify purpose and begin to move, we tend to gain a new and stronger life urge. This in turn affects how we relate to others. In going over your letter, I was delighted to read what you said about beginning to regain your love for people. It reminded me how I often find that my tendency to love or not has a lot to do with my own being state. When I feel good about myself, I tend to have much more tolerance and concern for the people around me. I believe that getting ourselves into the process of becoming helps us feel both more productive and more loving. Feeling productive and loving has a lot to do with having influence and impact.

∽

In my last letter I included my life statement. The first three paragraphs were about my purpose. The first paragraph makes a strange assertion that I will live in the creative or extraordinary being state. The other two paragraphs provide some elaboration, as you'll see if you review that letter. You will also notice that I don't identify any specific goals.

When I was younger and worked on clarifying where I was going, I used to set specific goals, such as projects I would complete by a specific date. I wanted to accomplish certain concrete outcomes. I still think setting clear goals is important. I recommend that you put yours down on your life statement. I no longer list my specific goals because I want to stay clear about something I tend to keep forgetting.

Although achieving goals is exhilarating, we can also get obsessed with them and miss one of life's great secrets. A major payoff for human effort is the process of becoming, of growing as we move toward our goals. I remember the day your basketball team won the state championship. We were walking out of the Breslin Center at MSU. People were still celebrating wildly. You turned to me and said, "I almost feel bad that it is over. It's like I'm already missing something." I think you were sensing that you were going to miss the *work* of becoming a champion. There is joy in the efforts and relationships of purposeful work. There is joy in the process of becoming. Life seems most meaningful when we are progressing toward our goals and growing into a more capable person. At those times I often find that I am in what, in my life statement, I call the "extraordinary being state." This state is one in which I tend to have a feeling of great well-being. It is also a state in which I find myself relating to others in more loving ways that seem to elevate those others. Here I would like to share some thoughts on what I think it means to be extraordinary. Let me tell you a story.

When I was a boy, Grandpa once came home with a puppy that we named Candy. When she was very little, Candy became sick. Though it seemed certain for a time that she would die, she miraculously survived. Perhaps that brush with death had something to do with the personality she developed.

Physically Candy was not very attractive. In fact, if you just looked at her, you would probably say she was ugly. Yet Candy had a most unusual characteristic. She loved to see people. In fact, when she met someone she knew, she would become a bundle of enthusiasm. Instead of wagging her tail, she would wildly wag her entire body. She never jumped on anyone or did anything irritating. She, like Snoopy, just ran circles around people while her whole body communicated her happiness. Her enthusiasm was infectious. Candy made people feel that they mattered.

Everyone who met Candy reacted positively. My friend Bobby Suggs used to say that he had been scared of dogs until he met Candy. Candy changed his outlook. Even the mailman looked forward to coming to our house. It was the high point of his day. The insurance man used to come by once a month to collect his money. When he came and Candy was not around, he wanted to know where she was. Seeing Candy was as rewarding as getting his money. Walking down the street, Candy would approach complete strangers with that same expression of joyfulness. Even the coldest and most aloof person would seem to melt in the presence of her warmth.

As I said, Candy was not much to look at. But I think everyone saw her as attractive, maybe even beautiful. What came from inside her altered the image people saw when they looked at her. And because Candy did not behave in an ordinary way, people had to stop and make sense of her. Since she was so excited about seeing them, they concluded that she cared about them. They thus became attracted to Candy and responded very positively. Candy was extraordinary. She had influence. She changed people! Candy was what you might call a "positive deviant."

Over the years you have often heard me say that there comes a time in our lives when we need to choose to be extraordinary. I am not sure I ever explained exactly what I mean by this. Think for a moment about the concept of the bell curve. Statisticians often employ the bell curve, and you've taken classes where you were graded on the bell curve. At the middle of the curve is the mean, the average, the most typical score. The curve is shaped like a bell—hence its name. It is highest in the middle because that is where most scores—the average ones—tend to be. The farther you move from the middle, the fewer and less typical the scores will be. For example, if the mean or average score on a spelling test turns out to be 70 on the bell curve, then most of the people in the class must have scored between 50 and 90. Only a few will have scored below 50 or above 90.

The bell curve has other uses besides portraying the distribution of test scores. Given a random sample of people, it can reveal the distribution of a common characteristic among them, such as speed, age, intelligence, strength, or beauty. The middle or high point of the curve will disclose the mean or average amount of the personal characteristics sampled. Meanwhile, the lower and higher parts of the curve depict its lesser or greater presence. The bell curve can be used to describe the performance of anyone in any situation. At the far left, at the low point of the curve, we would find people whose performance is very poor. Usually these are people who are disadvantaged, ill-prepared, or rebellious. In society people who live at this lower end of the curve are often given negative labels—criminal, prostitute, and so forth. Sociologists have an entire field of study devoted to this subject. Usually the second course taken in sociology is called Social Deviance, a concept I'll return to in a moment.

Most people find themselves placed in the large middle area of the bell curve. One week they are just below the average, the next they are just above it. The intensity and quality of their efforts vary according to what's going on in their lives. In fact, it has often been shown that they meet the expectations that exist; that is, if they know that people around them are expecting them to score low, they will score low, and if the people around them expect them to score high, they'll score high. A kind way to describe the performance of most people is to call it "average." A less kind but equally accurate word to describe it is "mediocre."

Where the curve slants downward at the far right we find a very different group. These select few stand out from all the others. They are people who are especially effective. They have become unusual. I like to call them the "positive deviants." They breach expectations in positive ways.

I've sometimes thought there should be a third course in sociology called Positive Deviance. But the one time I used that term in the presence of a sociologist, he was offended. He insisted that deviance, by definition, is negative. There's a lesson in this—that social scientists tend to study the middle of the curve (normal behavior) or the left side of the bell (deviant behavior). They focus little attention on the right of the curve (positive deviance or excellence). Only in the past few years have we seen the birth of a field called "positive psychology." At Michigan, we are presently creating a related effort called "positive organizing." We are trying to achieve a better understanding of the dynamics of positive deviance.

I have always been interested in how to live on the right side of the curve. I am particularly interested in the issue of how an ordinary human being, one with human limitations just like us, can *choose* to become extraordinary. I believe that most people who might otherwise be classified as average can choose to become extraordinary. Talents, past experience, training, and environment are indeed important factors that can limit our performance, but it is possible for most people to move more in the direction of the right side of the curve.

On a sports team, for example, average athletes compare themselves to others, put in the same effort as everyone else, and then go home. By contrast, world-class athletes examine their diets, lifestyles, theories, techniques, and time allocations. They search for the small improvements that will make a difference in their performance right now. In doing this, these athletes leave the path of least resistance and forage into new territories. Here there is uncertainty, learning, and often painful change. Most people do not want to leave the path of least resistance. We seem to want to stay in our comfort zone, the place where we are in control and where we initially experience the least pain.

The athletes who leave the path of least resistance, or the comfort zone, become extraordinary. They step outside the middle of the bell curve. This is when they begin to experience real change and real progress. The athlete begins to explore and expand, growing in ways that are well beyond the average. Over time the extraordinary person following the extraordinary path changes inside and ends up no longer the same person as when he or she started out.

By definition, "extraordinary" means just what it says: "extra ordinary," above and beyond the ordinary. That is what we think when we watch a world-class athlete. We watch the external performance and conclude that this is why this person is extra-ordinary. We are wrong. What we are viewing is the product or expression of what makes the person extraordinary. But the truth is that such people are able to perform in extraordinary ways because of what they have on the inside. They have the capacity to commit to being their best self and to pursuing that commitment. They have a hunger to grow and develop. It is because of what they have on the inside that they can behave in slightly different ways that others can observe. That's where they make an impact on the world. That's where they make a difference. That difference originates in the will to grow. When we make the effort to move toward the best self, we make a change in our being state. This is the essence of what I call a "being change." As Robert Fritz would say, we gain a "new and stronger life urge."

An extraordinary person keeps examining self in relation to some higher purpose and keeps striving to conquer and move beyond the limits of that self. None of us can ignite our potential by staying on the path of least resistance. We find meaning and power when we extend ourselves in the service of something greater than ourselves. When we are experiencing victory over self, we become conscious of our own unique value and become joyful and influential because we are *positive deviants.*

I want to clarify something here, that being extraordinary does not necessarily mean obtaining a position of honor or glory or even of becoming successful in other people's eyes. It means being true to oneself. It means pursuing one's full potential. Interestingly, I believe that when we fail to do this, we actually do ourselves damage. We begin to die inside, and we hate ourselves for our decision to kill our best self and live as an ordinary self. I think we are designed to be extraordinary and that when we fail to pursue being extraordinary, something begins to crumble inside. We move to the middle of the curve, and our ordinary self prevails. We may even move to the left of the curve and begin to get depressed because we are not growing. We are designed to be growing, and when we are not, we violate the purpose of the universe. We fail to live on what I call the great upward spiral of life.

I have a colleague in India who interviewed Mother Teresa. He asked her how she came to have such an impact on the world. She answered, "I invested great love in a very small thing." When I think about those words, I cannot help but think about that petite

young woman sitting in the front row of the Michigan undergraduate class, who asked, "Who is going to listen to anything I say?"
The answer is "It all depends." Mother Teresa also was small in
physical stature. So how could it be that a small, very ordinary
(at the outset) woman like her, surrounded by the poor masses
of India, had the profound impact on the world that she did?
She did it by behaving in an extraordinary way. She was a positive
deviant. Her investment of great love in a small thing changed the
world. Extraordinary things are done by ordinary people who
choose to behave in extraordinary ways.

    I believe that all extraordinary people are ordinary people
who chose to do extraordinary things. They become extremists in
the service of some purpose. When Michael Jordan played his last
game for the Chicago Bulls, the TV people asked him if his friend,
Charles Barkley, might be the next star to win an NBA championship. In essence, Jordan said, "I do not think Charles has the
discipline to pay the price."

    Note that he did not say that Barkley lacked the talent.
Barkley had extraordinary talent. He was at the far right of the bell
curve. Theoretically he was certainly capable of leading his team
to the championship. Yet compared to the ten best players in the
league, his talent was more ordinary. Jordan was suggesting that
talent is necessary but not sufficient. Jordan was saying that
Barkley was not an extremist in the service of the collective goal.
An extraordinary person is clear about the goal, brings all his or
her talents to that goal, and combines those talents with extreme
commitment. Jordan, for example, had the reputation of being
one of the best practice players (working hard in practice) in the
history of the NBA. Larry Bird was the same way. Extraordinary
performers are ordinary people who become extremists; they pay
more than their peers are willing to pay. They invest more of
themselves willingly and enthusiastically.

There is a danger in the example I just gave. I don't want you to think I'm saying that the measure of extraordinariness is winning or excelling in a competitive situation. That is one way to think about it. But don't forget that Mother Teresa was extraordinary, and she was not competing. She was working very hard to serve. Extraordinary people tend to have a purpose, but then they learn to love the process, the work, the grind it takes to achieve their purpose. In doing so, they grow to the point that they are unusual, positive deviants.

The most important way for you or me or anyone else to be extraordinary is to be loyal to our best self. We have an ordinary self. It is the self that exists when we are in the comfort zone. Our best self is very elusive. It exists only when we are in the process of becoming more than we are. As soon as we stop becoming, we enter the comfort zone, and the best self slowly *devolves* into the ordinary self. Then, after a period of time has passed, we begin to yearn for something we may not be able to identify. We may become depressed. You see, I'm convinced that we all need to grow and learn. It takes courage to grow and learn, so we are sometimes more loyal to our ordinary self than we are to our best self. When we are loyal to our best self, we grow into the unique person the universe is training us to become as the universe attracts us along life's upward spiral.

The process sounds noble, but there are hidden hazards. If we choose to be a positive deviant, we are by definition deviant. Deviants are deviants because they are not in the middle of the curve. As deviants, we violate the expectations of other people. We encounter social resistance and pressures to conform. In elementary school our classmates may tease us for getting good grades. Many bright kids then stop pursuing grades. Positive deviants choose to leave the path of least resistance, and in making this choice they experience adversity or loneliness. Adversity takes many forms and is a critical issue.

I once read a book called *Adaptation to Life.* It was a forty-year study of Harvard graduates. The researchers tracked every aspect of the graduates' lives. Since they were all Harvard students, they all tended to get good jobs and make money. By this standard, they were all successful. Yet they were not all the same. They fell into two very distinct groups. The study found that everyone experienced adversity—bad things happen. What separated the two groups was their response to adversity.

One group coped with their bad times by engaging in self-defeating behaviors. The other group coped with their bad times by using positive coping mechanisms. For example, let's say that a man from each group lost his wife. One man would cope by drinking heavily. The other would cope by writing love poetry, memorializing his deceased wife. The first coping behavior is self-defeating. The second is a positive coping mechanism.

This may sound like a small difference, but I think you'll see why it is also very important. The self-defeating group turned out to be less happy, less healthy, and likely to die sooner than the group with positive coping mechanisms. Those are crucial differences! How we cope with adversity matters. The old adage "If life hands you a lemon, make lemonade" isn't just a clever saying; it's an important principle. Another way to say it is "Bloom where you are planted." Whatever our situation, and no matter how bad the cards we are dealt, we need to know how to handle our response patterns. We need to know how to make a being change, a change in our state of being. It is a fundamental change in how we are. If we change how we are, we change who we are. That is what Shauri did when she wrote her life statement.

If we choose to clarify purpose and move toward the right side of the normal curve, we are making a being change that will call forth our best self. Now here is an important point: the choice to call forth our best self changes the external world in which we exist. I want to share a story with you that illustrates this point.

When your mother and I were first married, I was in graduate school and had a very heavy course load. Yet I needed to earn enough money for your mother and me to survive. I knew I could not do it on the minimum-wage jobs available in a college town. I decided that I would work for the Fuller Brush Company. This meant going door to door and selling brushes and other home care products. Selling door to door is difficult because it means experiencing rejection many times a day. Each night I would leave the apartment at five, drive to the neighborhood, and sit in the car. Hating what I was about to force myself to do, I would drag myself to the first door. I would usually do about ten doors and get ten negative responses. Finally I would stop and tell myself that I was wasting my time.

It was tempting to tell myself that I had been assigned a bad neighborhood. But I was also experienced enough to know the problem was the not the people. I was the problem. I was following a normal script and getting normal results. I was not willing to step out of that normal script. I needed to make a being change.

In that situation I had a trick I would use to help me make such a change. I would stand on my toes, close my eyes, squeeze my fists, and bounce up and down until I could feel the energy flowing. Then I would run, not walk, up to the door and knock. (Sounds silly, but it always worked.) When people came to the door, I would bowl them over with positive emotion. With great enthusiasm I would hand them the free sample of the month and tell them how glad I was to be of service and ask how I could help them the most. Most nights I would make sales at seven of the next ten doors. No matter how many times I tried this, I was always amazed at how well it worked.

Why did it work? Why did the same kind of people who had been rejecting me suddenly become good customers? What was different, the people or me? Obviously, it was me. If it was me, then there is an important implication. I was in control. The normal assumption to make is that the people in the houses are in control. They can choose to slam the door or invite me in and let me demonstrate products. An ordinary person in an extraordinary being state alters the routines of the people encountered. The choice to call forth our best self changes the external world in which we exist.

Now there is a paradox worth noting here. We can make two seemingly opposite arguments: one, that the world controls us, and two, that we control the world. Actually both are true. Under normal circumstances, an ordinary person knocks on a door and gets an ordinary reaction. The world is in control. When a person is filled with enthusiasm, as I was, he or she is no longer ordinary. When that person knocks on a door, the situation is no longer normal, nor is the response of the person who opens the door going to be ordinary. The residents of these houses will have to come out of their routines and be mindful. They have to figure out what is going on. When they have to be mindful, they have to open up to the situation, to react in a unique way. When they open up, they feel the enthusiasm. They feel positive emotion. The core positive emotion is love. Instead of being repelled by their fear (a negative emotion) of what we represent, they are attracted into a positive relationship. When it comes to enthusiasm, when we move to the right of the curve, the world tends to change.

Now there is one thing I do not like about the preceding example. The example is about sales. In sales, people often talk about *techniques* for manipulating people to buy. This tendency leads to a false conclusion that goes something like this: "We need to be positive thinkers so we can manipulate people to do the things we want."

When I was selling Fuller brushes, I had one motive in mind—to make money. I was there to sell and earn a living. Now notice that as long as this was the primary motive, I failed in my intention. I did not make money. I did not sell very much. I was an ordinary salesperson generating ordinary or predictable outcomes. When I took control and went outside my comfort zone, I became more inner-directed. That's the being state where something else happens. We become more other-focused. We become more concerned about the needs of others. The person who answered my knock was no longer a neutral object who was going to buy my products and pay me money for them. Rather, I was now glad to see this person and was there to "serve." When my purpose (making a living) was supplemented by a focus on others (love), things changed.

The jump from self-focus to other-focus is not easy to contemplate. Self-focus is so central in our world that it is hard to even imagine an other-focused being state. In sales training, management training, and many other forms of training, self-focus tends to dominate. We make the assumption that we must be *in control* and pursuing our own interests to the exclusion of anyone else's interests. Because sales instructors make normal assumptions, they end up teaching techniques for manipulation. What they say may sound logical, but it never quite works.

Now let's look beyond this to what happens when we become inner-directed and other-focused. What happens is that we seek to serve people. We establish relationships in which we are not in control. Rather, together we cocreate the future. To do this, the other person must be honored and free. And we must be honored and free. When we choose to enact the best self, we invite people into relationships of love in which we explore the paths to a mutually enhancing purpose. We serve each other and grow. We sell the new mop or the new car not because we cleverly controlled the customer but because we brought something into the customer's life that would fulfill a genuine need or a desire that the customer already possessed.

This concept of giving up control is hard for people to understand. Few people experience it because few people are willing to exert the effort necessary to alter the routines in which they live. It is natural to resist a change in our being state. I think of a time when you were little. It was Halloween. You went up to every door and said, "Trick or treat!" This is what every kid was saying at every door. It was the ordinary thing to do. I tried to give the routine a different slant.

"Why don't you try something different?" I said. "Go up to a door and say, 'Hello, I hope you are having a wonderful evening.' I'll bet that before the night is over you'll get twice as much candy as anyone else."

First you told me what you thought of my idea. You were not exactly enthusiastic. A few minutes later, I mentioned it again, and you said, "OK, fine, I'll do it." What that meant was "I'll do it and show you how good your dumb idea is!" You walked to the next door totally disgusted. You came back disgusted. You held up a single candy bar and said, "See, one candy bar, just like every other house!" That was the end of that.

So what exactly does this illustrate? It illustrates that many people are unlikely to experience what I am talking about. They want to stay inside their normal routines. They become actors following a script. The normal expectations are the script. The script then keeps people from seeing other possibilities. They do not understand that enthusiasm changes things. They also fail to understand that they can increase enthusiasm by simply choosing to do so.

Someone once said that the definition of insanity was "hoping for different results while doing exactly what we have always done in the past." If a person is unhappy, the only way to stop being unhappy is to behave differently. Right now! This is difficult because there is a script in your head that says this is how

I am supposed to behave in this situation. But guess what: we can behave differently only if we choose to violate our own scripts. If my old script is a source of unhappiness, behaving differently at least raises the possibility that I might become happy.

Happiness is a function of change. Change your behaviors, and you will change yourself. When I change myself, I learn and grow. When I grow, I tend to become filled with enthusiasm. Enthusiasm means God within. When I *am* literally becoming enthusiasm, the people around me are touched because they feel what I radiate. They feel positive, attractive, loving power.

I want to issue a challenge to you. It is even more difficult than the one I gave you on Halloween many years ago. The challenge has both a general and a specific aspect. First, at the general level, I challenge you to be at least as influential as my dog. She had positive impact on everyone she met. Bathe people in enthusiasm, and the world will change for the better. Enthusiasm is a choice, not an accident. So the general challenge is to bathe people in positive energy.

The specific challenge is to pay special attention to people. Your job in the universe is to change people, to increase the meaning in their lives. That means everyone all the time. So many people relate to others in normal but ineffective ways. They look for others to care for them in some way. When others do not care, they feel disappointed. The normal way to live is to be externally driven and self-focused. The extraordinary way to live is to be internally driven and other-focused. The latter is truly a productive being state.

You may be thinking, "He's asking me to be a phony." That's an important objection. But here is my argument. The extraordinary image does not reflect the ordinary feelings we may be having at that moment. So in one respect it would not be authentic behavior. However, if we followed that logic further, it could mean that the only way to be authentic is to stay in one's current scripts. This limited notion of authenticity would require that we never grow. So how do we solve this puzzle?

We recognize when people are being authentic because they are not just routinely following the normal scripts. Authenticity surprises us because authentic individuals know who they are and do not always behave in the socially prescribed way. Such people are internally driven and usually other-focused. They are more authentic than others because their words, behaviors, feelings, and values are more congruent.

You, like me, tend to be introverted. People often think of enthusiasm as a characteristic of extroverts, like your mother. But I believe enthusiasm knows no boundaries. Even though I tend to be an introvert, I often feel enthusiastic. When I go into a classroom to teach, I often make the choice to change my being state. As I become clear on my purpose to change the lives of my students, I become more focused on identifying and addressing their core needs. I gave you an example of this in the first letter. In that state I tend to be enthusiastic. I am filled with positive emotions. At my core there is both purpose and love. The students feel and respond to me. I believe it is then that I am most authentic, the real me, the best me.

If you were to take my challenge seriously, you would see that all the people around you are prospects for using your influence to elevate them. You would accomplish this by bathing them in enthusiasm. You would do it by finding positive ways to take them out of their everyday scripts. You would seek to help them grow. You would not be *kissing up* to them or manipulating them because you were in fact being authentic. You would be clear that you are an enthusiastic person in pursuit of a higher purpose. You would be behaving in ways that are not normal because you are not normal. You would never have a conversation without finding a creative way to sincerely express positive emotion.

If you did these things, you would notice a most unusual thing. You would notice that people are drawn to you. They would treat you in ever more positive ways. They would send you signals that you were a positive deviant and that they were glad that you had the courage to persist in the face of their resistance. You would begin to notice that the world is comprised of good people doing good things. This would be true because you would be a good person doing good things. But I must warn you that other people would put great pressure on you to revert back to the normal state. Positive deviance always makes some people uncomfortable. You would resist this pressure because you would be addicted to the rewards of positive deviance. You would notice that you had credibility, that people listened when you spoke, that you were no longer an emerging leader but a very powerful leader. You would notice that you were as authentic, as influential, and as happy as my dog Candy was. That would be a significant achievement and a reward in and of itself!

Love,

Dad

Pursue Your Best Self

Dear Garrett,

I am glad you enjoyed the last letter and were able to focus more. I agree that taking notes as you read is a great idea. It will allow you to identify the things you resonate with. It will also allow you to respond more fully and thus increase your own learning. You wrote something that I found very striking:

> *Reading the first few pages of your letter made me think of Coach Townsend. He is almost always in the extraordinary being state. He is a gifted man, but the impressive thing about him is the way he makes the most of his gifts. Did you know that when he was young, he had dyslexia? It was a huge problem for him. He had lots of failures and took a lot of heat, but he refused to quit. He made it all the way through college. When he told me that story, it blew me away. You have to respect a guy like that. It is surprising to see how many times I think about him. He has had a lot more impact on me than I ever realized.*

I agree with your observation about Brian Townsend. He is a good example of someone who lives in the extraordinary being state, and he does make the most of his gifts. I did not know about his overcoming dyslexia. That may help explain why he is so good with people while he is also committed to achievement. He understands that coaching is about discipline and winning, but he also understands that it is about relationship and caring. He is internally directed and other-focused. And he has another key characteristic: he is absolutely committed to learning. He reads constantly, watches training films, and goes to sports clinics. In fact, Brian is more open to feedback than any coach I have ever met. When he first took the coaching job, the criticism was that he was a football player and did not know basketball strategy. Four years later, you could put his command of strategy up against that of any coach in the country. At the end of last season, his critics were saying that he was losing all his talent and this year he would have a bad record. I looked at the paper the other day, and the team is 7 and 1. People who live in the extraordinary being state tend to succeed, but even when they don't, they learn. Then they succeed. I think I have some clues about why Brian is the way he is.

A few months ago we had some people here for dinner. Brian and his wife, Rachel, were included. In the conversation I brought up the notion of being internally driven and other-focused. Brian seemed to think carefully about the concept and then told two stories. He said that when he first arrived at Michigan as a student athlete, the football experience was incredibly competitive. He worked intensely to please the coach and get playing time. This went on for four years. In his fifth year he had an insight: He had to play for something other than the coach. He stopped worrying about what the coach thought. He said this was a defining moment in his life. From then on, he became internally driven. If he was with the team watching game films and the coach complimented him but Brian felt he did not execute perfectly, he noted what he had to do better. If he was criticized but felt he did well, he gave himself a pat on the back. He became his own coach. He was now being internally and not externally driven. He described it as one of the biggest breakthroughs in his life. It was a point of high joy. I think he was joyful because he had become internally directed; Brian was creating a more joyful Brian. He was creating and discovering his best self.

After a couple of years in the pros, Brian was grinding it out in practice one day. He suddenly noted that his pro experience had been joyless. He asked himself why he was there. The answer was clear—money! Without realizing it, he had made an invisible shift. By becoming money-driven, he had moved from being internally driven to being externally driven.

He said, "I grew up in an African American family of six boys, and to survive, it was always family first. When I went to Michigan, the thing that made Michigan special was that it was team first. In the pros, everyone was playing for himself. I realized that a critical value was missing. In the pros, my motivation had changed. I try to take that lesson to what I do now. In basketball, that is what I am about—building a real team, a real family, moving my players from self-interest to a higher level of motivation. That gives me joy because it allows the boys to experience joy."

Brian is in the business of helping boys find their best selves. A day or two after our conversation over dinner, there was an article in the *Ann Arbor News*. It was about Amani Toomer. You probably remember he played football for Michigan. He was a second-round draft choice, but in his first three seasons for the New York Giants, he caught only forty-four passes for 635 yards. His major contribution was on specialty teams. Then, in the 1999–2000 season, he had seventy-nine catches for 1,183 yards and six touchdowns. That broke the team record and put him among the best in the NFL.

One of his teammates said, "Something was holding him back his first couple of years. But whatever it was, he found it, that's for sure." He was clearly highly talented and highly skilled, so what changed? What made the difference?

Here is one clue: the writer of that article describes watching Toomer in practice. A pass is thrown near his feet. He misses it, and a defender throws him hard to the ground. He walks back to the huddle staring at his hands and repositioning them at various angles. Later he explains that he was actively trying to envision how he could have made the catch. He was telling himself what he would have to have done, under game conditions, to protect the ball.

The writer points out that such behavior was not the case previously. Toomer was always making mistakes and was always in the doghouse. Yet between 1998 and 1999, he seemed to commit himself. In the off-season he greatly intensified his work efforts. In this last off-season, Toomer did more long-distance running to extend his stamina. He took up kung fu to extend his flexibility. He found a personal trainer to work with, and he further increased his involvement in the team's off-season training program.

Brian Townsend says that one of the biggest breakthroughs of his life was becoming internally directed and learning to work for excellence and the love of the game. For Toomer it was the same kind of thing. He had to become internally motivated. As he committed himself to the grind of the work, he grew, and as he grew, he found joy. "You have to fall in love with working out in the off-season. You have to fall in love with training camp. You have to try to keep the intensity up and never forget what got you where you are. I just want to keep building." These are the statements of a person with purpose and the commitment to learn and grow. Such people are continually in the extraordinary being state, and they are continually in contact with their best selves. They succeed because they are able to look very carefully at their old patterns and try new ones until they find ones that work. They do not get into the rut of hoping for different results while always doing what they have done in the past. As you have observed, "That is insane—but it is so easy to be insane!"

You raised an important question in your last letter. It relates to all of this, and I think it is great. You said that you were struggling with motivation. You commented that while you agreed with things in my letter, you were having difficulty putting them into action. You tell yourself that you should do what I challenge you to do, and you think that you will, but then you put it off, knowing that you'll never get back to it. You said you were having a lot of trouble responding to challenges, though you had never had this problem in the past.

A key point here is that you never used to have this problem of not responding, but now you do. I agree that this is probably true. At Thanksgiving when you were home and banged up the car, you were feeling pretty bad. You said, "For seventeen and a half years my life was great. The last year my life has been awful." I think you're correct there, too. I remember in the fall of your senior year, when you were elected homecoming king, your brother Shawn made an interesting observation about you. He said, "The rest of us work so hard, and Garrett just seems to flow through life, yet he is incredibly successful!"

I think Shawn is right. For most of your life you have attracted people and success. But then in the past year you have really struggled. So what is the difference? In your first letter you suggested a possible explanation: you said that school is not interesting to you, that you like to sleep and some people say you are depressed. You also commented that you were "beating yourself up."

Once again I think your observations are very accurate. You do seem to be depressed. You say you sleep too much. You feel irritable. You lack energy, and your self-esteem is low. When people say, "I am beating myself up," that usually means they are feeling guilty. All of this and your inability to concentrate sounds to me like depression. Here are some things to consider.

First, depression is not something to be ashamed of. It affects more than seventeen million people. It isn't a weakness of any kind but a medical disorder, like having a cold or a broken arm. Depression can be brought on by specific events in our lives, or it can seem to emerge for no apparent reason. A normal person who has a broken leg or continuous severe headaches would not hesitate to get medical assistance. But for some reason, when we're depressed, we say to ourselves, "If I want to, I can pull myself out of this." Such thought processes keep a lot of people stuck. They hope for different results while they continue in their old patterns. Again, that's a pretty common thing to do.

The second point I'd like to make is that depression has become fairly easy to treat. There are a lot of medications available today, and they are both safe and effective. With most of these, you have to take them for two to eight weeks before you notice much improvement. There are a few caveats that go along with taking these medications, like staying in touch with your doctor, continuing the medications as prescribed, maintaining regular social patterns as opposed to being alone, and eating and exercising in healthy ways. And finally, avoid alcohol and drugs.

Given the struggles you are having, I suspect it could be worth your while to see a doctor. In fact, I have been sensing you are on the verge of doing so. I say this because I realize you are already making progress. Each time I talk to you on the phone, you seem a little more positive. I sense that you have more of an inclination to recognize the problem and more of a desire to do something about it. If it would help, we can locate someone for you.

I think the critical thing at this point is to take some action. If you start breaking out of the depression, you will find it far easier to concentrate, and you will be more likely to try some of the new patterns I am suggesting in these letters. I think this may be part of the answer to your question about challenges and motivation. But of course, there is more.

I want to tell you to pat yourself on the back. In your letters to me you have taken up the challenge by trying out new patterns. Talking openly about this stuff, for example, is a very positive new pattern. So you have made progress, though you might not yet be able to see that you have. I think it's difficult to stop and consider what is good about what we have already done. We underestimate our own accomplishments. I have always found it important to reflect on what is good about what we are doing. That acknowledgment is a potential source of strength.

You may remember that in my life statement I described my "best self" characteristics as well as what I call my high-performance profile and my high-performance roles. When I start to lose sight of my sense of purpose, I find these statements extremely helpful. The problem is that life sometimes seems as if it is designed to keep us from knowing our best self. It would be easy to go through life without ever being clear about our best self. Let me tell you a story.

Bert Whitehead is a financial adviser. My partners and I invited him to consult with us as we considered the next moves in launching a company. Bert is no ordinary finance guy. He defies all the stereotypes. That day was no exception. He began by telling us that as entrepreneurs, we should run our lives so that we have 180 days a year free of any work obligations. That statement seemed absurd but certainly attractive. We listened as he explained his philosophy and followed up each of his theories with statements that demanded our attention.

Finally he got to his key point. He told us that all three of us were unique and masterful creators of value. We were where we were because we could create value. He also explained that each of us was *incompetent* at some things. He then asked us to identify our areas of incompetence. We made our lists and presented them.

Next he said that we were each good to excellent at some things and asked us to identify those. We did. Then he said we each have some skills that are unique. We use our unique skills to create value in extraordinary ways. He again asked us to identify these, and we did, or at least we thought we did.

Bert then spent some time talking about how success breeds failure. That really got our attention! He said we succeed because of the skills we have developed, but our success leads to new expectations. We get drawn away from our high-value-added activities and get trapped into doing things we are only good or even incompetent at doing. The key, he argued, is to structure our lives so that we are spending as much time as possible using our unique skills to create value. We were just starting to agree with him and to accept these ideas when he moved on to his next shocking assertion. He told us the lists we made were not any good. He told us that we were self-deceptive and could not trust our own lists of unique skills. He then gave us our homework assignment: we were to contact some of the people who know us best and ask them to help us identify our unique skills. All three of us were uncomfortable with the assignment. I decided that if I was uncomfortable about it, it was probably worth doing.

After the meeting, I went home and made a list of about thirty people from different areas of my life. There were family members, longtime friends, and professional colleagues. Some came from the past, others from the present. They shared two characteristics. They all knew me well, and they were people who I knew would give me their honest opinions. I then sent them all e-mails explaining the assignment I had been given and asked them to share some feedback on how I most create value or what my unique, positive characteristics seem to be.

The responses started to roll in. I read them with great interest. In fact, I could not put them down. There were about thirty-five responses. Some were very brief. Some were very long. Some told stories. I saved them all because they told me things about myself that I did not know. Those insights energized me in new ways.

I had often received formal feedback, but it was usually pretty superficial compared to what I was getting here. This feedback was rich, and it was focused on what people most valued about me. I found it almost overwhelming. Why? It was an intense form of appreciation.

Look "appreciation" up in the thesaurus and you will find four streams of associations: approval and positive reception; thanks and gratitude; understanding and awareness; rise and elevation. All of these seem applicable to what I was experiencing as I read these statements over. In reading what these people had written, I felt approved and received. I felt thanks and gratitude. I felt that people understood me and were aware of the best parts of me. I particularly felt elevated. The feedback simultaneously humbled and uplifted me; it made me want to be my best self as often as possible.

There was more. As I pored over the responses, I was struck by something else when people gave examples of particular incidents: helping a woman understand her daughter, telling a story in a department meeting, teaching in a certain way, not getting mad at a woman for disagreeing with me, asking an angry administrator to tell us what we were doing wrong and thus opening honest communication. Most of these incidents I had long forgotten. Even when they occurred, I did not think of them as particularly unusual. I was just doing what seemed like the natural thing to do at the time. I thought it strange that much later, people would remember these incidents and place such great value on them. To me, all of these incidents that marked what they felt were my unique contributions seemed very commonplace. It was stunning to me that people would assign such importance to them.

There is another interesting thing. As I read through the statements, I noticed a great deal of overlap. People seemed to recognize my patterns of value creation in fairly consistent ways. This surprised me. People in very different contexts were seeing my best self in the same way.

I took the responses I received and began an analysis. I pulled out all the descriptive statements and tried to organize them. I spent many hours creating categories. Gradually a structure began to emerge. I originally had five pages of analysis. Finally I boiled the analysis down to the following statement.

My General "Best Self" Characteristics

In enacting my best self, I tend to be creative. I am enthusiastic about ideas and craft bold visions. I am an innovative builder who perseveres in the pursuit of the new. I do not waste energy thinking about missed opportunities or past failures, nor do I take on the negative energy of the insecure, nor do I worry about the critics. I do not waste energy in defensive routines. I stay centered and focused on what is possible and important.

I have frameworks that allow me to make sense of complex issues. I get to the essence. I can see disparate ideas and integrate them through "yes-and" thinking. So I make points others do not readily see. I tend to be inner-directed, so my message comes from an authentic level. I think deeply and speak with conviction. In doing so, I frame experiences in compelling and engaging ways. I paint visions and provide new ways for people to see. I use metaphors and stories to do this. I find the stories in everyday experiences, and people find it easy to understand them. The new images that follow help people to take action.

In helping others, I see the possibility for greatness in people. I calm them while I energize them. I help people identify their own core ideas, core emotions, and core values, and it has a catalytic effect on how they feel and think. They see

*new possibilities, and the excitement helps them find the
courage to act. I give them my attention and energy, but I
allow them to be in charge.*

*In exercising influence, I do not try to think others into
action. I try to enroll them in new directions. I try not to sell
but rather to invite people into my journeys. In pursuing the
journey, I seek reality. This means seeking honest dialogue.
I do not get defensive or reject others if they are uninterested
or if they choose to focus elsewhere. I make it clear that the
relationship is more important than a conflict, and honest
dialogue will improve things. At such times, I surrender my
ego and invite criticism.*

*As a teacher and interventionist, I do not seek to inform
but to transform. I use dialogue to help people surface their
ideas, and then I weave those ideas together with others until
we create knowledge in real time. In doing so, I move them
from the abstract to the concrete and from the objective to the
intimate. I ignore symptoms and focus on the deep causes.
I ask piercing questions. I help people and groups surface the
darkest realities and the most painful conflicts. From these
emergent tensions comes the energy for transformation.
I liberate people from their fears and help them embrace new
paths. In all of this I try to model the message of integrity,
growth, and transformation.*

There was something about these statements and the analysis
I did that was unusually powerful for me. Previously I made lots
of assumptions about my strengths. Yet I had never asked anyone
how he or she saw my strengths. To do so had seemed unaccept-
able because to me it violated the norms of humility. What these
people gave me in their statements was unusual and made a
unique impact on me. Every time I reread these pages, I feel

energized. The appreciation and love of the people making those comments seems to pull me out of my ordinary patterns. I become filled with energy and want to initiate new projects. I feel elevated and motivated.

There is another reason why this feedback was so powerful. It was not just that people were appreciating me. There was something else. The information provided was not about my ordinary, reactive self. Usually we focus on our weaknesses and failures. I tend to spend plenty of time seeing myself negatively. So do you. So does everyone. When we do see ourselves negatively, our self becomes a problem to be solved. This very personal information was about my successes and my contributions. It was about when I was adding value. All of this gave me hints about my purpose and how I best enact my values. All of this material tended to pull me into the realm of possibility and hope. It provided me with clues for making a greater and more positive difference in the world.

As powerful as the process can be, however, I've become increasingly aware of some hidden incentives in our lives that work against it. Usually we use feedback about ourselves as a way of identifying problems so we can work on them. It is amazing how pervasive this problem-solving perspective is. Purpose-finding seems so innocent. Yet it upsets people because the world is married to problem-solving. The world is a reactive place, and purpose-finding is not about reacting.

When we begin exploring purpose-finding, the issue of humility comes up. Identifying the ways we do well is viewed as a form of bragging. It is prideful. I surely have been guilty of pride and will be again in the future. When I am prideful, when I brag about something, it is usually because I feel insecure. I feel the need to impress someone. I want others to admire me, and I am manipulating them.

But this process of getting feedback from other people about what makes me unique was quite different. The feedback made me feel that I sometimes do make a positive difference. It also made me feel connected to other people. I could feel love and appreciation in their words. In the connection and love, I could feel a form of greatness. Not greatness from within me, but greatness moving through me.

I remember a speaker quoting John Ruskin: "The first test of a truly great man is his humility. I do not mean by humility, doubt of his own power. But really great men have a curious feeling that greatness is not in them but through them. And they see something divine in every other man and are endlessly, foolishly, incredibly merciful."

Here is how I interpret this quote. Humility–being humble—is often associated with weakness or lack of power. Real humility comes when we see the world as it really is. The real world is a world of connectedness, of moving flows of power. When we transcend our own egos, when our outer self and our inner self connect, we experience increased integrity, increased oneness, greater connectedness. At such moments we feel greatness. Yet we recognize that the greatness does not emanate from within us, as we assume it does when we brag. It emanates from connectedness with resources outside our conscious self. I think that is one of the things that best-self feedback demonstrates to the person who receives it. Our greatest added value tends to be contributed when we are doing the things that we do naturally when we are in caring relationships and in pursuit of a genuine purpose because we are connected to unconscious gifts.

In discussing this idea with a friend, he repeated something he was once taught by one of his spiritual mentors. He said that the mentor told him:

Each of us has a little piece of the creative force within us. But what you must come to realize is that this is a sacred gift and it does not belong to you. It is the Creator's way of working through you. So get the heck out of its way! To block it or not allow it to work through you is sheer narcissism, and you have a responsibility to serve the creative force in every way you can. The most generous act humans are capable of making happen when they are open to this gift and express themselves through the resources it offers.

I think he really understood what I was trying to say. I think a key to having that force move through us has to do with purifying our motives. Remember Shauri's comment that clarifying her purpose meant "purifying herself"? Purifying oneself means learning to live from increased integrity and love. When our best self is operating, that is how we are behaving, not out of pride or arrogance but for the good of the task and the relationship. When I act with this kind of authentic commitment, I am strongly motivated for the good of the system and not for my own aggrandizement. That is when my greatest sense of connectedness occurs. At such times of connectedness, what I sometimes call "profound contact," we become aware of the best in others and in ourselves. They love us and we love them. We then extend ourselves in others' behalf; we become merciful, forgiving, and full of love.

It seems to me that the feeling of humility emanates from seeing things as they actually are. It is feeling the awe of connectedness and abundance. It is experiencing the connected self. As such times we become clear about who we are. We see both our shortcomings and our strengths.

Humility is knowing that despite our shortcomings and our strengths, we are dependent on the universe for our every resource. Humility is recognizing that we flourish only in connect-edness. Since I often forsake connectedness, I often lack humility. Most of the time I am not in touch with my authentic self, my best self. Most of the time I pretend to be humble in the way society expects me to be. I am continuously reacting to assumed expecta-tions, pretending to be what I think people think I should be.

I occasionally enter a more authentic state in which I tran-scend myself. I make profound contact with someone or something in such a way that I am then filled with possibility. At such times everything seems different. I feel incredibly strong but also feel that I am but a microscopic entity in the vast universe. I am aware of both my vast potential and my complete nothingness. I suggest that at such times I am in some sense modest, meek, docile, and sub-missive because I feel connected. I am *at one* with some kind of universal reality or power. I feel nothingness because my self tends to dissolve. I witness my total dependence. I discover that despite all my self-deceptions, the truth is that I am not in control. I am a process, and I live in a universe of constantly changing parameters. Yet I can live successfully with a universe of change, and that gives me a higher kind of control. It is at such times that I am moving forward on the upward spiral of life.

This awareness does not turn me into a weakling. To the contrary! It makes me feel incredibly confident and strong. I feel empowered and empowering. I sense that my best self is who I really am meant to be. My lesser self is not truth but temporary error. *My best self is the real truth.* To see things as they really are is to see that fact. I cannot see it if I am not humble.

Scott Peck wrote about humility in *The Road Less Traveled.* He was discussing something similar to the enactment of the best self, the process of becoming masterful and experiencing *true power.* He said when true power happens, a person experiences the joy of increased awareness and increased joy. People also experience humility because they "experience a diminution of their sense of self." Peck says this loss of self brings with it "a kind of calm ecstasy, not unlike the experience of being in love."

Meanwhile, the everyday world will say to me, "You need to know what you need to improve, not what you do well." In making that statement, society assumes that life is about problem-solving. Who we are is problematic. Our being is filled with problems, and we need to solve them. Here my mind returns to the notion of purpose-finding. I thought about Shauri writing her life statement and then changing her outlook. In that act Shauri was creating a brand-new self, a purified, best self. I thought about you and this exchange of letters. In them I see you slowly moving toward your best self.

Sad to say, most of us are never taught to prize and honor our best self. So we do not. It takes a conscious choice to do so. In searching for and finding our best self we change, and the quality of our relationships changes. Being change is leading change. If we change our own being, it changes the people around us.

We live in networks. We exist in relationships. When we bring our best self into a relationship, things change. They really do. We are stretching to give the best we have. Those are moments of purposeful love. If we offer our best self, we offer love. When we feel love, we feel hope and envision a brighter future. If we commit ourselves to pursuing that brighter future, we are no longer reactors in life. We become creators of value. In relationships where we do this, we automatically provide the leadership for the relationship, group, or organization to move forward.

We tend to enact the things we think about. If we think about the normal self, that is the self we will seek to create. If we focus on our best self, that is the self we will seek to create. Bert Whitehead's exercise, which I discussed earlier, is designed to teach us to recognize and pursue our best self. In essence the exercise is asking,

"What do you love about me?" Once we have the answers of others, we can get up our own courage to ask the countercultural question "What do I love about me?" I think we almost never seriously entertain that question. When we answer it, when we become aware of our own positive core, appreciation escalates, hope grows, and courage expands. We see our real self and thus experience increased humility, real humility. In encountering our best self, we encounter the creative force that energizes the universe.

When we love ourselves in the positive sense I am exploring here, others are then more attracted to us. They trust us. And often this trust is something they can't even define. They want to join with us in the pursuit of meaningful purpose. When trusting relationship is joined with meaningful purpose, relationships, groups, or organizations become more willing to sacrifice for the newly envisioned future. They feel empowered and empowering because they are no longer locked into their problems. They are more ready to pursue the results they want to create.

After going through the process Bert showed us, I asked myself why I was so fascinated by the feedback I received. Why did I have so many new insights? Why did I want to initiate new projects? By getting input from others on how I best created value, I had surfaced important information about my best self. The ideas in that feedback were positive. They were also real in that they came from my own history. They triggered new ideas in me that helped me integrate the old best me with the possible future best me. These were insights that integrated my past and future and tended to unleash my pent-up energy. The process made me feel empowered, and I wanted to act. With growing confidence I was being drawn toward the possibility of new relationships with new purposes.

When people give us appreciation as they did here, when people love us, it brings out the best in us. Many people around us appreciate and love us, but they do not have the opportunity or the inclination to tell us this to our face. And we certainly do not have the opportunity to ask. To ask means stepping way outside the box. Many people, for a variety or reasons, will simply not do it. At the business school, I have started using this process with executives. When they get their best-self feedback, they have all the same reactions I had. What they find most amazing, I think, is that the people in their lives actually love them. Under normal circumstances there is no way for them to know this. It sounds strange, but think about it. Life is structured to prevent such communication.

I urge you to consider this experiment for yourself. Ask for some feedback about your best self. If you are tempted, write a short note explaining some of the things I discussed here, and tell people you would like them to share some feedback about your best self. Ask them to think of some times when they watched you add unique value to some situations. Ask them to tell you briefly about those situations and to identify how they think you add value. Send the request to as many people as you can think of. Review the names in your e-mail address book. As the e-mails come back, save them in one file. Then copy that file and begin to break the responses into categories. Then capture the essence of each category. Then write a statement that integrates across categories so that you can easily focus on the whole.

I would hope that I would be one of the people you'd ask for such feedback. So I would like to be bold and give it to you right now.

In one of your letters you mention that you have God-given gifts. That is true. You particularly have a brilliant mind. When you were little, it came across before you ever went to school. You seemed to excel at things your older siblings were struggling to do. In school the teachers immediately started to confirm this.

I remember when the fourth-grade teacher wanted to move you into eighth-grade math. He said he had never had a student like you. One of my favorite manifestations was when your older brother was doing his homework. He would read some complicated math problem out loud, and before he could finish the last sentence, you would look up from the TV and call out a number. He would say something like, "That's stupid." Then he would work on the problem. Five minutes later he would say, "I can't believe it!" Because the answer you'd given had proved correct.

The place where I most noticed your brilliance was in coaching you over the years in the recreation basketball league. When I was coaching the fifth graders, you were in the third grade but played well with the fifth graders. I would call time out and put in some play. You would offer some alternative, and I would ask why. You would give an explanation, and I was always astonished at how much sense it made. You could see things that most people could not see. I think that is still true today. You can see things that most people cannot see. You add great value because of your capacity to analyze and see what is going on around you.

Your second great strength is your capacity to love. When you were a baby, you had the capacity to love people. You and your brother Travis were both very little. He would work himself into great frustration and then curl into a ball and suck his thumb. You would go over and pull his head in your lap and sit there twirling your finger in his hair. The two of you would sit like that for ten minutes at a time. That pattern went on for years. In a similar vein, I remember when you were in the first grade. The teacher said, "I have been teaching for twenty years. I have had a few students who have been as bright as Garrett. But I have never had a student who was as bright as Garrett and who was also as skilled socially. If he finishes his assignment, he walks down the row, finds someone who needs help, and then sits down and works with the person. In most cases that is a recipe for disaster. Not with Garrett. Every kid in the room wants to be with him. They all love him."

I remember taking pictures before one of the proms. One of the mothers said, "Are you Garrett's dad?" I answered yes. She said, "All the girls love Garrett because he treats them so well. He is a very caring person." Another example is when you first started dating. You found out your girlfriend's father had some issues because he fought in Vietnam. You came to me with the deepest interest and asked me to explain what Vietnam was about because you really wanted to understand him. What followed was one of our best conversations. You care about people in a deep way, and they feel it. You add value because of your capacity to love.

The third characteristic is also related to love. You tend to have few ego needs. You do not seek aggrandizement. You usually take your victories and your losses in stride. In the first two basketball games of your senior year, three of the five starters were ineligible. The team needed points. You delivered in a big way. I remember noting that and saying that you might have an impressive scoring average by the end of the year. Clearly you were capable of doing so. Your response was, "That is not my job. My job is to get the ball to other people, to help them score. When everyone is back, that will be what I need to do for the team." You were not making a big thing of it. You were just stating the fact that your job was to get the ball to others. It did not bother you in the least. I think deep down you have a wonderful sense of who you are. You are not externally driven. You do not need to impress people. You add value because you operate without ego needs.

Finally you have the capacity to greatly focus your energy. This was particularly exhibited in the state tournament during your senior year. As the tournament began, you intensified your focus more than I have ever seen it. At the end of the district and regional championship games, you cried uncontrollably. It was not from the joy of winning as much as it was the release of an incredible level of intensity. In the quarterfinal game it looked like the game was over at halftime. In the third quarter you picked the team up and willed them back into the game. It was the best quarter I have ever seen you play. Losing that game was a big blow. Your focus was astounding. When you find a purpose, you are capable of making great sacrifices in pursuit of it. You add value by making those sacrifices and helping others reach their dreams.

You add value to my life just by talking to me. I love to have meaningful conversations with you. I love getting your responses to these letters. I love you and I want you to know it. You are a magnificent human being.

Now, I realized that most people are not going to have the courage to ask others for best-self feedback. Asking would just be too far out of the box for them. You may feel that way yourself; I don't know. So there are at least two other ways to identify patterns associated with your best self. One is called a high-performance profile. Mine reads as follows:

My High-Performance Profile
When I am at my best, I tend to enter a meaningful situation that has the potential for increased synergy and long-term impact. I do not intrude. I am invited in because of perceived competence and credibility. I am integrated with a caring associate who tends to logistics and execution. I seek to understand the implicit processes and structures that drive the system. I search for the single bold stroke that will transform the existing paradigm. As I do so, I tolerate ambiguity,

explore the parts, and conceptualize the whole. These grounded observations allow me to communicate images with confidence and passion. People feel and see alternatives. I seek to both relate in a loving relationship and to challenge with high standards; in other words, I seek to be empowered and empowering. In doing so, I facilitate the creation of an emergent community of empowered people. Toward the end of the experience, I yearn for new stimulation and seek to manage the transition and movement to a new adventure.

A high-performance profile can be created without asking anyone for feedback. It is a process I learned from a colleague, Jerry Fletcher. Jerry wrote a book about how to generate and use high-performance profiles. Here is his brief overview of that process: "An episode of high performance is a time when you experienced a high level of success." Ideally the episodes you identify would come from different aspects of your life—sports, social life, work, church, school, and so on. You identify the episodes, and then you write the story that took place in each case. You try to write each of the stories in some detail. You include how you got the episode started, what kept it going, and how it came to an end.

Once you have written the stories, you do a cross analysis of them to find themes that they all share. In asking how you get your high-performance episodes started, for example, you look for commonalities in the starting process in the stories. If in one story you notice you did something that seemed important, ask if you also did that in the other two and just forgot to include it. If you notice a given pattern in getting started, you simply write a line that describes it. Here are some examples from how I get started: "When I am at my best, I tend to enter a meaningful situation that has the potential for increased synergy and long-term impact. I do not intrude. I am invited in because of perceived competence and credibility. I am integrated with a caring associate who tends to logistics and execution." There are no right answers. Every sentence of a high-performance profile is unique to the person writing it.

Once you have written a high-performance profile, it can become a great aid for turning future projects or events into high-performance events. When you get stuck and start to feel depressed, you can examine your profile. You can check to see if you are in some way outside that profile. Is there something you can do to change yourself or the situation so that you can get back into your high-performance pattern?

A similar technique is to list ten or twenty of your best life episodes. Here you do not need to write the stories. Just make a list. Then ask, "When I am at my best, what roles do I tend to play?" By way of example, here are my answers:

My High-Performance Roles

I am at my best when I play one or more of the following strategic roles.

Explorer: I seek personal and collective enlightenment at the edge of chaos.

Point guard: I seek to make the aggregate more than the sum of its parts.

Interviewer: I listen for the underrepresented collective voice.

Visionary: I conceptualize the unspoken need.

Facilitator: I bring to the surface the truth that is too painful to be engaged.

Storyteller: I attract people to change by sharing images that enable.

*Role model: I attract people to change by achieving and
    exposing an authentic self.*
Leader: I attract people to change through being change.

These are the roles I play when I am making the most difference.
Notice that many of these overlap or are confirmed by the descriptions people gave me for my best-self feedback. When you have
outside confirmation like this, it is a good sign. If you attempt to
identify your best-self characteristics in several different ways, you
should begin to see themes.

The list you make of your own high-performance roles can
be used just like the high-performance profile. It becomes a list
you can return to when you are stuck. You can ask yourself if you
need to change the way you are behaving. Would you be more
successful if you moved to a role that you play particularly well?

In writing these letters I have been trying to focus on influence and impact. In life we tend to get stuck in our comfort zones.
In our comfort zones we get trapped into problem-solving. We
end up living a reactive life. This reactive pattern can get so bad
that we become depressed. The challenge, then, is to start where
we are. If we are depressed, we need to see a doctor. If we are not
depressed but trapped in our comfort zone, we need to continually
clarify our purpose. The challenge is to understand that life is
most meaningful when we are in the extraordinary being state.
We get there when we are growing, experiencing victory over self.
When we experience victory over self, we encounter our best
self. Some people, like Brian Townsend, are very good at spending
time in the extraordinary being state. It is here that they work

hard, like Amani Toomer. They are exercising discipline and finding joy in the difficulty. The joy is a manifestation of moving toward purpose. It is a sign of growth.

It is important to understand our own unique way of creating value. The better we understand it, the better we can pursue it, and the more often we can make a difference. That is what influence and impact are all about. I think you are beginning to move toward increased influence and impact. I think you are beginning to answer your own question about motivation.

I love you.

Dad

Maintain Profound Contact

Dear Garrett,

Thanks for the letter. It sounds like you and your sister Kristin are getting along well. That is great, particularly because you two are sharing the car. That is a definite challenge, and I am glad that you are managing it well. You wrote that you liked the story about Amani Toomer. In doing so you make some important observations:

> *I really enjoyed your last letter. The story about Amani Toomer was great, especially that part about falling in love with training camp. I think that it is so important to have a positive attitude about the work you do that nobody notices. If you work hard when nobody is watching, then eventually people are going to notice that you are performing at a higher level. My attitude in the off-season made all the difference in the world during high school.*
>
> *My freshman and sophomore seasons were mediocre because the team and I did not make the necessary effort in the off-season. There was little team spirit or commitment. Then Coach Townsend came, and everything changed. My junior and senior years were spectacular because everyone was in the weight room during the summer. They all worked out, built their strength and endurance. They were also serious about improving their skills. It's the same way with school. It's so important to do the little things, things other people don't even know we're doing. I guess it is the same with everything. Like you said, if you learn to love the grind, life gets better.*

The next part of your letter that jumped out at me was about depression. I went to the psychologist for the first time on Wednesday. It was a strange experience for me. I took a test, and he said that I fell in the "moderately depressed range." It was funny to me because the test seemed so stupid. I would have answered nearly all of the questions the same way at any point in my life. And I seriously doubt that I have been "moderately depressed" my whole life. The whole thing seemed like a joke. I felt like I knew everything he was going to say before he said it. I'm just not sure what to make of it all at this point. Maybe my next appointment will be better.

Maybe I am like Amani Toomer before he started to love the grind. Maybe I am not doing my part and blaming others. I am still struggling with my negative feelings, and I have a hard time getting things done. I procrastinate everything. I still just want to sleep all the time. I sleep a lot.

I think this passage is important because it illustrates an important tension: the difference between knowing and doing. You illustrate a mature understanding of the principles that result in growth. The problem is in the execution. In the past year you have lost the will to operate as you used to operate. We all do this. We all fail to live up to what we know we should be doing. We all get discouraged and sometimes depressed. When that happens, we get stuck and cannot move forward. At such times we really need other people to help us.

I was talking to Kathy Diehl, who, as you know, is a psychologist. She says that in working with depression, she continually stresses the need to maintain systems of support. It is important to be socially active, to have people to talk to. She said that we tend to withdraw from social activity when we're depressed. She tries to encourage people she is seeing to push to stay active in positive relationships. That is one of the differences you mentioned in your life. You used to love people, and more recently you have found that you are feeling much more negative about people. The one way to change that is to be disciplined about social activity. Discipline yourself to go out and to make and stay involved in social relationships.

You note that almost everything I write in these letters reminds you of things Coach Townsend said. That might be because these letters are about making an impact and having a positive influence on the world. That is what a great coach tries to teach his or her players, how to affect the world (in this case win) through personal discipline (bringing forth the best self) and collective cooperation (teamwork). In athletics, everyone needs to be his or her best self, and everyone's best self needs to be integrated with the best self of all the others.

By the way, I agree that asking for feedback about your best self from people who know you best can be scary. It violates the rules. Yet such feedback is extremely valuable for understanding how we make a positive difference. I loved this statement:

> What you wrote about things you have done that affected other people was interesting to me. I think about that a lot. It's amazing how much we can affect another person's life without even knowing it. I got an e-mail from one of my teammates recently that gave me a feeling similar to what you talked about. It came out of the blue. It was very touching. He talked about when he first met me and we first started playing together. He said he was jealous because I had such a neat family and so much support. His dad left when he was small, and he has always felt that life was a lonely proposition. As time passed, his feelings changed. He said he felt like he was my brother and a part of our family and so

*he did not need to be jealous. He told me how he felt about
me, and I was very touched. When I then got your letter,
it made me want to let people know how much they mean
to me.*

We often do affect people deeply, even by doing things we
think are small or not very important. I am glad you received that
letter, and I am glad you are enticed to let people know how much
they mean to you. If, as you say, people get caught up in trying to
be what others expect them to be, then sharing appreciation and
best-self feedback is a great way to make the world a better place.

I had an experience this past week that reminded me a lot of
you. I attended a meeting that focused on father-son relationships.
The people who put on the meeting interviewed a number of men
and then made a video of the interviews. Many of the men said
their fathers never expressed love for them. Many felt they had no
relationship with their fathers because their fathers were uninvolved in their lives. Many talked about these things with unusual
emotion. It was clear, decades later, that these men still carried
feelings of injury and even anger. Speaking about their fathers was
very difficult for them. I think most fathers fail to maintain a rich
emotional relationship with their children. Many children thus
never really know their fathers. They often feel deep anger about
this fact. Yet they grow up and become fathers just like the fathers
they had.

In a video they played at the conference was an interview
with a man named Richard. He talked about his father being a
good man. Yet his father was uninvolved in his children's lives. He
only once watched Richard compete in sports. He only twice took
Richard to the business the father owned. He just was uninvolved.
He felt that raising the children was the mother's job. His job was
earning a living.

In his college years Richard found himself very angry with his dad. In the years that followed, whenever he would go home, he and his father would end up in an intense argument within thirty minutes of his arrival. Finally a friend gave Richard some advice. He suggested that if Richard did not like the arguments, he needed to change his own actions. Richard started working on it. He stopped expecting things from his dad and found himself becoming less angry. Eventually there were few arguments at all. Then Richard decided to take more initiative. He became more disciplined about initiating open conversations with his father. This proved successful, and over the years their relationship improved dramatically. Now Richard reserves two days a year when he pays for a weekend in a hotel in a nice location for just him and his dad. He describes the wonderful discussions they have and how much their relationship has grown and improved. He says they have really come to know and love each other.

There are many reasons for valuing this story. First, it illustrates what children and fathers both want but often do not know how to get or give—communication and relationship. I think we all want to have a sense of profound contact. When we know each other deeply, when we love each other deeply, we have a sense of profound contact. In a relationship of profound contact, a relationship of love, we behave in ways that lift each other up. It is wonderful and far too rare.

Many people live their lives as victims. They feel angry with their fathers and abused and deeply wounded. Then they grow up and, as fathers, repeat the same patterns with their kids. The sense of separation between father and son goes on and on. People say, "What can I do? That's just the way the world is. I can't change it." In other words, they complain about the outcome while continuing to engage in the behaviors that produce that outcome. As you wrote earlier, we are all insane.

In Richard's story, Richard feels like a victim at first, but he makes a choice to change the old pattern by changing himself. He chooses to make profound contact with his father. He stops focusing on his father's faults, stops being a victim, and becomes a positive deviant. He moves to the far right of the curve and enters the extraordinary being state. He chooses to create profound contact.

One reason I like the exchange of these letters between you and me is that we are choosing to make profound contact happen. You and I are coming to know and love each other more deeply. I want you to know that I do love and admire you and that you light up and lift my life.

On my bookshelf is a video on golf instruction by Johnny Miller. I think you may remember me watching it while we were at Hilton Head. In fact, if I recall that moment correctly, I think you made some disparaging remarks about my golf swing!

The Johnny Miller tape is unusual. Normal golf instructors tend to focus on things like the proper grip, the right back swing, and the proper follow-through. Such instructors offer hundreds of "swing thoughts" to their students. Miller's approach takes a different focus. Miller tends to be preoccupied by the tiny fraction of a second when the club is actually in contact with the ball. In fact, he claims that he has spent much of his adult life studying this short moment of contact. He says he deserves a Ph.D. in the subject. Indeed, as I listen to his insights, he seems to have deep knowledge about the moment of contact and can talk about it in a way that is most helpful. One senses that he really is a masterful teacher with unusual wisdom.

It's the moment of contact that I also am interested in. What fascinates me is the moment—or maybe it's even the *episode*—of profound contact. This contact matters a great deal in life. If we can understand it better, we can improve something much more important than our golf swing. If we can master the notion of profound contact, we can live a life in the extraordinary being state where we are most likely to make a profound contribution.

I know a psychologist. In helping the depressed, she encourages them to discipline themselves to stay in positive social relationships. Well, everyone needs to stay involved in positive social relationships. The problem is that so many of our relationships leave something to be desired. Many are superficial, and many are negative. Profound contact is about creating and maintaining positive, mutually enhancing relationships. That is exactly what Richard did in the story I told about the father-son conference; he changed a negative relationship into a positive one. As a result, Richard is living a more positive life.

In the second letter you wrote to me, you indicated that you were getting busier, that you were feeling better about yourself, and that your relationships were getting better. You were feeling more positive about people. That is important because one of the most difficult things in life may well be maintaining good relationships. One look at the divorce rate confirms this fact. Marriages fail; courtships fail; friendships fail. When they do, it tends to hurt deeply. Some people never recover. A person rejected by a high school sweetheart may spend the rest of his or her life reacting to the event. Once injured, some people never allow themselves to love again. Psychologists say that the definition of mental health is the ability to work and to love. When we get depressed, for example, our productivity goes down and we tend to become neglectful of our relationships. On this point I sensed a big difference between your first letter and your more recent ones.

Almost since the start of time, people have been asking why it is so difficult to maintain positive relationships. One reason is that relationships exist in a constantly changing context. When the context changes, conflicts emerge in the relationship. Many relationships then fail because the people involved do not know how to think in a productive way about what's happening between them.

Here is an excellent case that Peter Koestenbaum, an executive coach with a background in philosophy, recounted to Polly La Barre in an interview in *Fast Company* magazine. He tells the story of a young couple. The husband was promoted and transferred to Cairo. He goes home and excitedly tells his wife, but she is not so positive. She tells him that she is not taking her new baby to Cairo. If he wants to go, he will have to go alone. It was a serious conflict. If he gave up his promotion, he would be forever resentful of her for destroying his career. If she went to Cairo, she would be ever resentful for his insensitivity to her and her baby. The only solution was to ask very fundamental questions. Is it *my* career or *our* career? Is it *your* baby or *our* baby? Are we *individuals,* or do we operate as a *team*? What are our values? Such questions are transformational. In asking these questions, each of them came to a new awareness. His career was important to her. His role in the family was important to him. Once these answers became clear, a change took place. Each one had a new definition of self. They went to Cairo, but they were able to make the decision without resentment because they were operating on a new and surer foundation. The *what* of the decision was less important than the *how* of deciding.

The conflict over Cairo could be any conflict faced by people in any relationship. It could be between you and me, you and one of your siblings, you and your girlfriend, you and a roommate. Life is full of such potential conflicts. We normally react to conflict by withdrawing. But we sometimes engage in arguing the facts and then start using leverage, power, and domination. This only contributes to sick relationships, haunted by power struggles and bad feelings. Each person sees his or her own needs pitted against the needs of the other person. Each assumes that the only solution is for one person to win and for the other to lose. To get to win-win requires a change in perspective.

In my first letter to you, I told you about the difficulties I faced during my first year in college. I kept asking what I should major in. I kept trying to solve that problem and kept getting nowhere. Then the question changed. I began asking, "Until now, what was the most meaningful thing I ever did?" That's when my problem disappeared. I instantly moved to a deeper level. I moved closer to my fundamental values and purpose. When we clarify our purpose, progress is inevitable. Because of that sense of progress, I had a "new and stronger life urge." That is also what happened to Shauri as she moved from problem-solving to purpose-finding. I think that is what is beginning to happen to you.

That is also what happened in Koestenbaum's story. The couple returned to their purpose—not to their individual purpose but to their purpose as a couple. They moved to a more fundamental set of questions: Are we *individuals,* or do we operate as a *team*? The logic of this situation doesn't end there. It forces us to ask still more questions: If we are a team, why does our relationship exist? If we have a greater purpose than self, what does that mean for this moment? What is our purpose? Are we committed to that purpose? If the answer is yes, how does that fact change our perspectives when it comes to our differences? What kind of couple, group, or organization are we? What kind do we want to be? What individual changes are we willing to make for our collective purpose? Such questions lead to the further clarification of values and purpose that can improve the quality of our lives.

In the story about Cairo, the two people ended up defining their roles "from the inside out," as Koestenbaum put it, of who they truly were. The couple gained a more mature level of commitment and a strengthened relationship. Their relationship grew even while they grew as individuals.

Koestenbaum makes some important observations. He says, "Managing polarities teaches us that there are no solutions—there are only changes of attitude." A polarity exists when there are contrary qualities, powers, tendencies, forms, and so on. So the couple's relationship had a tendency toward career and a tendency toward baby—contrary qualities that produced their particular polarity. Koestenbaum suggests that managing polarities is about first recognizing them as such and then considering the credibility of both.

Normal thinking typically does not adopt a polarity perspective. Instead, it takes an "either-or" perspective. Like the people in the Cairo case, it first assumes a win-lose conflict. The polarity perspective recognizes differentiations as legitimate but sees and values the connections between them. It seeks a win-win solution by moving to a deeper level of understanding. This is a more complex way to think. F. Scott Fitzgerald wrote in *The Crack-Up:* "The test of a first-rate intelligence is the ability to hold two opposed ideas in the mind at the same time and still retain the ability to function." In the social world such complex thinking often is accompanied by what we call a change in perspective, paradigm, or attitude.

Hence the emphasis is not on solutions but on *how* we are. It is on our attitude, our outlook, our being state. When we make a change in our being, we become more inner-directed and other-focused. We begin to recognize that we exist only in our relationships and that the quality of our relationships determines the quality of our lives.

Consider our relationship—yours and mine. Since we started writing these letters, I have noticed a change. When I talk with you on the phone, and when you were home at Christmas, we seem to communicate with more love. That, in turn, has increased the quality of my life. The more love I experience in my life, the richer my life is. I feel better about me and about others.

It took some effort for me to write the first letter to you, and I suspect it took some effort for you to respond. As we made these new efforts, we were engaging in new behavior patterns. The new behavior gradually led to a being change, and with that came new awareness. When we have an expansion of our awareness or consciousness like that, new possibilities open up, and we experience more profound forms of contact.

We all spend so much time in our lives engaged in superficial forms of contact. We would all live richer and fuller lives if we could increase the frequency of profound contact. Getting good at this process is important because it gives us a more positive outlook. In fact, profound contact takes me into the extraordinary being state where we encounter profound possibility. Profound possibility means that instead of living in a world of limited resources and unending conflict, we can choose to live in a world of expanding resources and continuous growth. We move forward on the upward spiral of life.

I like Koestenbaum's statement that "when you grapple with polarities in your life, you lose your arrogant, self-indulgent illusions, and you realize the joke is on you." There is so much in our normal, everyday lives that call on us to see the world selfishly. From the middle of the bell curve we see a Darwinian struggle. By that I mean that we see everything in terms of competition, illusions that are arrogant and self-indulgent. We want to win at all costs. In that state we are externally driven and self-focused. To move beyond these self-indulgent illusions, we have to grapple with polarities, and that is hard work. It means consistently redefining self, clarifying purpose, and looking at why each relationship matters. It means recognizing connection. It means recognizing the foolishness of self-centered behaviors. Our selfishness is a joke—a deadly, self-destructive joke, but a joke nonetheless.

I also like Koestenbaum's idea that "to get that message makes you a more credible human being—instantly." As soon as we stop problem-solving and start clarifying purpose, as soon as we let go of our self-centered illusions, we are transformed. We give up being externally driven and self-focused. We become internally driven and other-focused. Our influence then skyrockets. Shauri was a great example. One moment she was wallowing in self-pity, and the next moment she had reached a level of strength that was almost unimaginable. Instantly she became a more credible human being. The people around her knew something was different. They paid increased attention to what she had to say. By making a change in her being, she automatically and instantly became more influential, more impactful. She began to elevate the people around her, and her career took off.

In Koestenbaum's story, the couple made profound contact. I think you and I have moved our relationship to a more profound level of contact, too. The word *profound* means "very deep; marked by intellectual depth; deeply or intensely felt." When two people ask profound questions about their relationship, they tend to move to a greater depth of understanding. They get clearer about who they are, separately and together. Their feelings become more positive, and they make a deeper commitment to the relationship. They understand that their individual happiness is predicated on enriching their connection. People grow as they learn to make more profound contact with other people, but this means that we have to learn to think more deeply about relationships. We must become masters of relational wisdom.

You and I have watched a lot of college basketball on television. We often complain about how bad some of the announcers are. The bad ones tend to see only the obvious. They make observations that are superficial or just plain wrong. These are the ones that we would put at the left end of the normal curve. There are others that are more adequate in their performance. They do not offend us, but neither do they impress us. At the far right of the curve we sometimes encounter a master, a person who sees deeply. Such a person is Billy Packer. People may or may not like his personality, but in announcing a basketball game, he sees deeply. He pays attention to every cue and recognizes patterns before anyone else does. I am always impressed with his insights. No other announcer comes close.

We find people like the basketball announcers in every walk of life. There is the novice who only understands what happens on the surface. There is the person with ordinary expertise who gets by in an adequate way. Then there is the rare master, the person who understands what really moves the system. Our challenge is to be a master of life, to understand the dynamics of profound contact and profound possibility. When we accomplish those things, we can more frequently choose to enter the extraordinary being state, where we are more likely to make a profound contribution and feel good about who we are.

From this point on, I want to explore something that few people understand. I know you love puzzles and challenges, so here is a tough one. What was the most important date in the history of Earth? If you scour your memory and all the history books you have read, you will probably not get the answer. It is not in the history books.

The answer is April 4, 2063. According to the crew of the starship *Enterprise*, this was the day of first contact. It was the day that humans first greeted an extraterrestrial civilization, after which nothing was the same. More value was created on that date than on any other.

In the movie *First Contact,* the *Enterprise* leaves the twenty-fourth century as it pursues the evil Borg back to the year 2063. This is just after World War III, when much of Earth's population was destroyed. April 4 is the day that Captain Zefram Cochran launched the first ship to travel at warp speed. Cochran was an entrepreneur, a man trying to make money by creating value. Despite his straightforward intentions, his action had unintended consequences. It turns out that at that moment that Cochran launched his ship, a Vulcan ship on a survey mission was passing Earth. The instruments on the Vulcan ship picked up the warp signature left by Cochran's foray into space. This signature told the Vulcans that Earth was a more sophisticated planet than they had previously assumed. The Vulcans therefore decided to make contact with Earth.

We are told that the impact of first contact was astonishing. The patterns of human thought and behavior changed dramatically. Technological progress was greatly accelerated. All of humankind became united in the hope of a greater purpose and in the development of a better universe. Poverty, sickness, and war were eliminated. Thereafter, and into the future, April 4, 2063, was seen as the turning point in human history.

Unfortunately we are informed only about the stimulus and the outcome. The Vulcans arrived, and the universe changed. We are told nothing about the actual process of first contact. We are left to assume that all went smoothly. Yet we might ask, is it likely that such a process would be smooth?

In another film on the same topic we get some clues. In a film titled *Contact,* Jodie Foster plays Ellie Arroway, a young scientist obsessed with the notion of identifying communications from

other planets. After considerable effort, she identifies messages
from extraterrestrial sources. The moment of contact occurs. The
news of the great moment creates great uncertainty. Various radical groups begin to demonstrate. Governments seek to protect
their interests, and thus great conflicts arise. Businesses begin to
pressure governments for strategic advantages. Conspiring scientists seek to steal credit and to take over the project. The national
security agency and other government bodies begin to interfere.
In short, the idea of contact has destroyed the old expectations,
and near-chaos reigns as people begin to make sense of what the
new patterns might mean to them.

So let's put these two dramatic plots together. First, there is
contact with an extraterrestrial system. As our two cultures are
joined, there is much confusion, tension, conflict, and agony.
From this chaos, a new system emerges. The new culture is more
differentiated and more integrated than the original system was.
It thus has stronger internal characteristics (no war, disease, or
poverty) and greater capacity to make external contributions
(progress in the universe).

That is much like what happened to the husband and wife in
the story told by Koestenbaum. The context changed. In the new
situation there were life decisions to be made. The husband and
wife each pursued self-interests. This brought confusion, tension,
conflict, and agony. When they clarified the purpose and value of
the relationship, they increased their commitment to their marriage.

Both people grew and matured so that each one was more
sophisticated, more differentiated, honoring each other as individuals yet recognizing their participation in the relationship.
The two of them were even more integrated. The marriage was
transformed and now operated at a much more mature level.

The notion of extraterrestrial contact may seem fanciful.
The idea of marriage may seem far away. Yet my description of the

transformational process is important because it represents how value is actually created in our lives. I think of the big advances in life as occurring in the period in which two systems meet, inter- penetrate, and are transformed. Yet in our individual lives such contact is almost always perceived as dangerous. Because we live in fear of profound contact, we become very skilled at living in superficial relationships.

Profound contact is important, and if we thoroughly under- stand it, we can vastly improve the quality of our lives. For that reason, it's worth spending some time exploring the notion of contact, interpenetration, and transformation in some depth.

At the physical level, consider the acorn and the soil. The acorn drops from the tree, and soon the shell cracks. The nutrients in the soil and the protoplasm in the acorn begin to interact. They become one in a creative exchange. The oak tree, a new and more complex system, springs from the interpenetration. The same is true in human biology. The male sperm and the female egg are distinct entities. Yet they, like the acorn and the soil, become joined in one interacting system. When they interpenetrate, new life begins. The interpenetration of the systems brings about a profound transformation. Simple cells evolve into complex human bodies. The same is true in the movie plots I recounted. Two differentiated cultures meet, and to the extent that they are held together or integrated, a new, more complex culture emerges.

Transformation means a change in the condition, nature, function, or form of a thing. Transformation sometimes entails a dramatic contrast, conversion, transmutation, metamorphosis, or transfiguration. The alteration sometimes seems magical, miracu- lous, or beyond understanding. We tend to marvel that the oak tree emerges from the acorn and the soil, that our physical bodies emerge from the sperm and the egg. Such examples occur throughout the physical world.

There are several key elements in this process: differentiation, integration or interpenetration, and transformation. First, differentiation suggests that there are two discrete systems that we see as being very different and separate. The acorn is very different from the soil. The sperm is very different from the egg. Second, integration suggests that the differentiated systems become connected. The two systems interpenetrate; that is, they become integrated and interact in such a way that they become one larger system. The acorn becomes embedded in the soil, the shell cracks and interaction takes place. The sperm and egg join and become one new system. Third, transformation occurs. The interpenetration gives rise to an entirely new or emergent system. We see the new oak. We marvel at the new baby.

Differentiation, integration, and transformation are steps in a natural process. The process is represented not only in the creation of oak trees and babies but in all natural systems. Think, for example, about how we think.

A social scientist named Albert Rothenberg analyzed award-winning breakthroughs in fields such as music, science, art, and literature. He found a common characteristic in all the breakthroughs. In each case the initiator had what Rothenberg called a Janusian insight. Janus is the Roman god who has two faces and so can see in two opposite directions at the same time. Thus a Janusian insight is one where we notice the simultaneous operation of two opposing ideas or concepts.

Einstein, for example, said that the happiest thought of his life was when he was able to perceive that an object could be simultaneously moving and at rest. If we stand on a roof and drop our car keys from one hand and a rock from the other hand, the keys are at rest in relation to the rock but are moving in relation to the roof or the ground. This was the seed thought for Einstein's entire work on relativity.

Rothenberg discovered that each breakthrough he studied was initiated by the discovery of how two apparently opposing ideas or elements could be integrated.

In the study of human behavior, integration and differentiation are processes that are important in analyzing a variety of psychological phenomena. In decision-making performance, for example, psychologists speak of "cognitive complexity," the ability to differentiate and integrate concepts and ideas. (Remember Fitzgerald's statement: "The test of a first-rate intelligence is the ability to hold two opposed ideas in the mind at the same time and still retain the ability to function.")

The researchers who study cognitive complexity argue that people who are deeply experienced in a given activity have greater cognitive complexity as it pertains to their particular form of activity. So a brain surgeon has greater cognitive complexity about brain surgery than a dance instructor does, but the dance instructor has greater cognitive complexity about dance than the brain surgeon has. In each case the more masterful person sees things that the novice does not see. The more experienced person can also integrate differentiated things in ways that the novice cannot. Hence the master musician can differentiate patterns of music and integrate them in highly creative ways. Research shows that people with greater cognitive complexity in a given area tend to make better decisions and thus perform better than people with less cognitive complexity in the same area.

There is another way to say this. People with the greatest capacity to differentiate concepts and to integrate those concepts tend to add greater value in their area of expertise than other people do. They have the potential to add greater value to the larger systems in which they exist. When you were leading a fast break in a game, you could see opportunities that others could not see, and so you could do things others could not do. You had a more creative impact and were more able to change the momentum in a game. People used to say you were a particularly smart player. Another way to say it is that when it comes to basketball, you had a higher level of cognitive complexity. If, in contrast, someone handed you a musical instrument, you were in big trouble. You had little capacity to differentiate or integrate.

The processes of differentiation and integration are also important in human relationships. It turns out that effective leadership, for example, has a surprising quality. Early on, researchers differentiated between the notion of person-focused leadership and task-focused leadership. These two categories recognized that some people tend to show concern for other people and some tend to focus on getting things done.

For decades researchers analyzed the effects of these two styles. It wasn't until recent times that someone noted that some leaders use both. And it turns out that using both is a transformational capacity. Leaders create value by integrating task and person, by showing concern and support while also maintaining uncompromising standards of performance.

Here we should note an important point. It took very intelligent observers years to notice that effective leaders could rate high on both people and task orientations. The researchers held two differentiated concepts—stuck in the paradigm that you had to be either people-oriented *or* task-oriented. It was simply not natural for them to integrate the concepts. Hence they could not at first see the interpenetration, even though it was a central part of the phenomenon they were so carefully studying. Once again, it is difficult to see the integration of concepts that are normally differentiated, even when they are right before our eyes.

If integrating differentiated parts is the heart of creativity, good decision making, and effective leadership, it also comes into play with groups and organizations. Do you remember last Christmas when we were watching Duke play basketball? You commented that the team had not only great talent but also extraordinary discipline. They really were a team. That means that five players, each with their individual and highly differentiated talents, establish relationships in which their talents are integrated into a single system that can outperform most other similar systems.

I have seen the same thing in business. Successful companies tend to be more differentiated and more integrated than their less successful counterparts. It's been shown that as organizations grow, they evolve and differentiate into more and more departments or units—sales, production, human resources, and so forth. These units take on different characteristics in terms of their purpose, their structures, how they treat people, and how they orient to time. As these organizations become more differentiated, it becomes increasingly difficult to integrate the efforts of the various units. And yet there are many highly complex and differentiated companies that are also highly integrated, and these tend to be very successful.

I think that differentiation, integration, and interpenetration occur in all areas of our lives and are clearly of value. Yet like the movie *First Contact*, they tell us about the process after the fact.

They do not, as in the movie *Contact,* tell us about the painful tensions involved in the process itself. This is the natural pattern: when people look back on what happens, they cut out the account of interpenetration because they have difficulty understanding and describing it.

I know a man who spent the past twenty years building the family business. It has grown to be a sizable company, an accomplishment for which he rightly feels very proud. He looks upon himself as a creative leader with a knack for seeing into the technological future. Over the years he has made a number of risky decisions that have ended up positioning the company for significant growth. In spite of his many accomplishments, he does not see himself as a great manager who can keep all the details in place. Given this self-assessment, he made a decision to find a person to complement his strengths. He hired a woman to be president of his most important division. She has a detail-focused orientation and is hard-driving. My friend has been delighted with the results she has produced. The woman delivers the specified numbers quarter after quarter. Yet my friend has a problem. His brothers are also significant players in the business. Each of them sees this woman as the antithesis of the organizational culture they helped build, which has always been a place of innovation, caring, and stability. Her hard-driving, results-oriented focus does not go down well with them. They do not trust her, and they put enormous and continuous pressure on my friend to get rid of her. He finds the conflict very painful. I asked him why he endures the pain. His answer was very simple: "It's what is best for the business."

Now this man would never see his own role in terms of differentiation and integration, yet that is what is going on. He has chosen to differentiate by hiring a woman who operates in a way that is outside the normal expectations. Her way of working causes conflict, and so the differentiated systems (the woman and his brothers) want to pull apart. But they cannot; they are integrated by my friend's commitment. The conflict causes him much pain, but the organization excels because of it. He is willing to pay the price because he is authentically committed to the success of the company. If the company was headed by a less authentic or integrated person, the chances are that the woman would have been replaced. That would have been the path of least resistance. There might be less personal tension between the brothers, but the company might suffer as a result.

My friend is very clear about the result he wants to create. He knows his purpose, and he knows who he is. He is willing to make sacrifices to keep the differentiated parts integrated. That integration maintains profound contact or interpenetration. He is the mechanism that brings the acorn and the soil together, and as a result an oak tree is produced.

That is one of the things creators do. They do what they must to allow oak trees to come into being. For the couple going to Cairo, the oak tree was a marriage. At Duke the oak is a championship team. In business the oak is a more profitable company.

All of this describes the process of transformation. If we understand this process, it can help us live in the extraordinary being state. But I would not want to leave you with the impression that transformation always occurs, for that is not the case. Just as in nature, most acorns do not become oaks. Most marriages do not reach profound contact. Most basketball teams do not win championships. Most businesses do not move to the next level. Most fathers behave like the father they are mad at. People tend not to leave their comfort zones. They tend not to enter the extraordinary being state. Instead what we see is turmoil and self-interested conflict that results in destruction rather than creation. People do not know how to create profound contact, and there is no Johnny Miller to teach them. But maybe by exploring these strange ideas we might be enticed into thoughts and actions that foster profound contact. My dream would be that you and I might always live in a state of profound contact and continue to become more than we are.

Love,

Dad

Avoid the Negative Zone

Dear Garrett,

Thanks for your response to my last letter. You say that seeing mastery is inspiring to you. You want to become a master. You want to deeply understand and move systems. I believe that maybe everyone does. I think that is what those college students were telling me in that class I described in my first letter. They want to make a difference but feel frustrated. I think one reason people get depressed is that they suddenly lose their sense of purpose and any sense of profound contact. They do not understand or know how to move the systems in which they find themselves.

When I read your response, the first thing I thought was how much I wanted you to understand that you already are a master. In high school you deeply understood and moved systems. You were captain of the basketball team because you were both technically and interpersonally gifted. You were homecoming king because you operated effectively in the social system of the high school. You maintained a wide circle of deeply caring relationships, while you simultaneously maintained your own identity. You were a member even while you were unique. You integrated membership and uniqueness. You integrated competency and love. You have all the natural instincts and competencies of a master.

Yet right now you are between times. One of my friends refers to such times as a lull. Lulls can unnerve us because we equate them with inactivity or nonproductivity. Actually, though, the lull is like the rest between heartbeats. And without that lull, there obviously would be no beat! Miles Davis, the jazz musician, once observed that the silence is as important as the sound in music. The lull can be viewed in a very positive way. Change has its own rhythms, like the beat of the heart, and as we encounter a new cycle or rhythm in our lives, the lull is just going to be there—it's part of the system.

You are trying to figure out how to let go of an old life in which you were masterful. This is difficult, especially during the period when you have not yet found a new purpose or mission, a reason and a place to make a difference. You are in the process of learning what your new place will be and how your sense of mission and purpose will serve and be served. There are probably millions of people who are going through the same process in their lives on any given day. That's why knowing how to negotiate this territory is so critical. It is easy to simply misread the signs and feel that nothing is happening or even that we are failing rather than see that it's integral to every cycle of change. This is an important part of what I was talking about in my last letter, where I explored the ideas of differentiation and integration. That's the foundation for thinking about profound contact and profound contribution and how these are important to the person seeking mastery.

It is too bad that things didn't work out with your psychologist. You say he talked the entire second appointment and all you could think about was how much you wanted him to stop. I find that ironic. It certainly doesn't sound like he was a master. He did not know how to make profound contact. You could have been a very difficult case, particularly if you went in with a bad attitude. But I'm not saying you were, and besides, that's not the point. Whether you were or not, the burden was still on him. He is the professional. He is paid to be a master, to make profound contact with the people who come to him for help—even the difficult cases. Unfortunately, in all professions there are novices, journeymen, and experts, but few masters. It takes great commitment to be a master. It requires that we care enough to open ourselves up to painful feedback and that we exercise enough courage to experiment with new patterns.

I might have been more concerned about your breaking off the relationship with the psychologist except for the fact that I get the sense that you are becoming increasingly positive with every choice you've been making. Your developing and maintaining more positive social relationships certainly shows that. I feel confident that you are slowly finding yourself. I suspect that being with Kristin has been helpful, and so have the new friendships you've been making. All of these interactions help break up the habits we all get into during periods of depression. You are beginning to experience victory over self and living in a more joyful being state.

I'm also concerned, though, that you monitor yourself where your feelings of depression are concerned. If you continue to have the kinds of discomfort you were talking about a while ago, realize that you can get some professional help and in particular some medicine to help balance your body chemistry. How would you evaluate your symptoms at this point? Are your feelings of depression lessening?

I am glad you liked the story about Richard changing the relationship he had with his dad. It seems to be a great illustration of profound contact. I have been thinking about it a lot. I think about the times in our lives when we feel and act like victims, when in fact we have an alternative. We can understand and change the system that we are complaining about.

In the letter you had some interesting things to say about relationships. You particularly mention the Cairo story and also the difficulty of maintaining relationships with people who are far away:

The part of your letter that struck me the most was the story about the couple moving to Cairo. It made me think a lot about how easily a relationship can be destroyed if there isn't good communication. I think it is very easy to forget how important our friendships are and our other relationships with other people are and how they can be affected by how we handle challenges like that couple had. If they hadn't taken the time to think the whole thing out and come to the strategies and insights they did, there would have been a lot of hard feelings for a long time.

I'm trying to keep solid relationships with the people I care about. But to be honest, this is proving to be difficult at times. I'm so far away from the people that I care about the most. I miss you and Mom. I miss Travis a lot. I also really miss Sara. We have been so close for three years. I miss seeing her smile. I miss touching her hand. I miss not being near her. We have had lots of conflict, like your story about the Jodie Foster movie, but we are pretty close to one another and it hurts to be separated.

Your comments remind me of two challenges: first, how to make these relationships meaningful, regardless of the fact that you are separated geographically, and second, how to always surround yourself with meaningful relationships in your present surroundings. You noted yourself that relationships can be easily destroyed, and it takes considerable personal mastery to maintain profound contact with the people in your life. Doing so, however, is the very key of abundant living. By choosing to invest in our relationships, we determine the course of our own happiness. Which brings us back to a familiar issue—clarification of purpose.

I recently had a dream that I want to share with you. In it I was a young man, and I was joining some important cause. After getting involved in the cause, something went wrong. Pursuing it took me places I did not want to go. That is all I remember, no details, just that theme. Nevertheless, the dream was so troubling it woke me up and I couldn't go back to sleep. I suspect it has to do with the work we are doing to get our new company funded.

If we get funded, everything will change. Dramatic and unpredictable new expectations will be placed on us. We will be required to engage in new behaviors as we move forward with the business. We will be caught up in a raging river that will change who we are. Going through such change is always quite frightening because it destroys the old you. You no longer know who you are. I am sure this is the reason many people do not go forward in their lives. I suspect the change from high school to college has been something like that for you.

I once knew a man who was brilliant. He came up with many great ideas. Yet every time he was on the verge of success, he would do something stupid, and the opportunity would go away. I watched him do this so many times that I became convinced he was afraid of success. That fear led him to sabotage all of his own most important life projects. He desperately needed to stay in his comfort zone. He did not have the courage to venture forth into the realm of uncertainty and allow himself to grow into the next level of who he was meant to be.

In these letters you may have noticed how much emphasis I am putting on purpose-finding. It is important to find a higher purpose and pursue it. This is particularly true in times of transition, like the one I am going through and the one you are going through. In transition our growth and happiness are dependent on the clarification of purpose. If we are very clear about the result we want to create, that clarity of vision may be powerful enough to attract us outside our comfort zone.

Yet my dream suggests a problem with the pursuit of purpose. I think I know what that problem is. It has to do with values. Values drive behavior. We value safety, so we lock the door at night. We value money, so we take a job. We value health, so we exercise. We make decisions based on our values. In making sense of the world, we do so through the values we hold to be important to us.

There is a downside to being value-driven. The first is that we have to make trade-offs between competing positive values. Some people call these *polarities* or *oppositions*. For example, with the couple who faced the problem of moving to Egypt that I talked about in the last letter, the wife focused on her baby and the husband focused on his career. Baby and career were both positive values. In that case they became competing positive values.

So much of life is like this. There are almost always polar tensions. For this reason, most of the great teachers in history have paid attention to polarities. The great teachers from China and India were very aware of polarities, and many of their teachings were focused on how to handle paradox. The ministry of Jesus also asks us to look at the paradoxes that affect our lives. The better we understand positive tension, the more we are able to see the need to consider both baby and career.

Unfortunately, our thinking is usually more superficial. We make quick decisions based on our values. We develop rationales to justify our values and our actions. If someone calls our values into question, we get very upset. It is particularly upsetting if someone can make a case for an opposing positive value.

In the dream I described here, I argued for purpose-finding and courage. But there is a polar perspective to that position, regardless of how admirable it may seem. Sometimes we leave our comfort zones and commit ourselves to a seemingly noble cause. In the process something nearly incomprehensible happens. The positive value we were pursuing gets paradoxically inverted into a negative one, and our pursuit of that cause begins to destroy us.

A visible example in recent years is found in the debate between pro-choice and right-to-life advocates. Defending the right to life is a noble position. Yet certain right-to-life extremists advocate life but also advocate killing doctors who perform abortions. The obsessive pursuit of life takes them to murder. They advocate a positive value, but their behaviors reflect values that have transformed from a positive to its negative opposite. The blind pursuit of a value tends to lead to the destruction of the pursuer.

Recognizing paradox and inverting values is a subtle process. For example, I might be irate because of the rampant dishonesty I perceive in government. In pursuit of honest government, I decide to run for office. In the process of looking for people to support me, I form many relationships and make many trade-offs. By the time I am elected, I am entrenched in certain interests and opposed to others. Over time I tend to get corrupted and end up just like the politicians I had committed myself to replacing. Yet I have become blind to my own corruption.

Now, it is easy to pick on politicians. And it is easy to look at a husband and wife who are having an argument and see how narrow-minded each one is being. What is difficult is looking at ourselves. When we are destroying ourselves by the narrow pursuit of a single positive value, it is very difficult to see our faults. We have too much invested.

Mark Twain once said, "It isn't what you don't know that will kill you, it is what you know that isn't true that will kill you." I return to this statement often. Our comfort zone is often defined by what works for us. When someone suggests an alternative, we get very upset. After all, why change something that works? We might even recognize that the other person is correct but cannot let ourselves consider the person's position because we are so sure of our position and assume that only one way can be correct. In some cases we are overcommitted to our position.

Recently your mom and I were driving over to pick up some friends. I started to turn left on a given street. As I did so, your mother shrieked, "No, go straight!" This happens occasionally and is always unnerving. Well, I had already made the turn. What followed was an animated discussion about which was the better way to go. It was not very productive. One route may have been only a few seconds faster than the other. Yet we both clung to our opinions that our own way was best.

In graduate school, a doctoral student must form a doctoral committee to guide the dissertation. Typically the student will seek advice on how to proceed. One faculty member will say, "You must do A, B, C." The student goes to the next faculty member who tells him, "You must do B, C, D." And the next person will answer, "You must do C, D, E." There may be overlap between the answers, but the answers are different. All this is confusing to the student. What makes matters worse is that each faculty member is convinced that he or she is the only one giving the correct advice. Why are they so convinced? Because they did their own dissertation that way and it worked.

As you know, I've spent much of my professional life trying to help people get better at seeing alternatives. Years ago one of my colleagues, John Rohrbaugh, and I developed a framework of competing positive values. It suggested that organizations are most effective when they integrate competing positive values. That is, the effective organization would be both very differentiated and very integrated. Since then I have expanded it into many other areas. In recent years, Kim Cameron, Jeff DeGraff, Anjan Thakor, and I have again extended this model.

We made up a word for what we do: *Wholonics.* I like the word because it suggests a vision of the whole. It's the notion that we can transform differentiated parts into a new, usually more complex, and effective whole. We wanted to create a tool for examining tensions within any system, identifying the positive-negative pressures, and then redefining negatives into positives and looking

for ways to integrate the opposing positives. The exciting thing is
that as we saw how well this framework operated for large organizations, it also became clear that this could be a model for our
personal lives. Picture a framework with four quadrants that
describe different forms of action (see the accompanying figure).
We've labeled each quadrant with an action verb (*compete, control,
collaborate, create*), reminding us that a healthy, dynamic system is
always moving and changing. In the figure, we consider the four
quadrants in terms of basic motives.

Compete (lower right quadrant): In life we all have an underlying need for achievement and power. Here the emphasis is on
achieving things in a world of scarce resources and abundant
competition for those resources. We often have to compete in
order to achieve. To get an A grade, a student has to outperform

The Wholonics Model of Basic Motives.

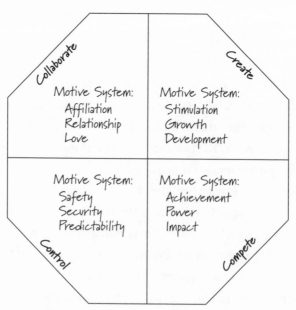

others in the class. To win a championship, a team must outperform its competitors.

Control (lower left quadrant): Throughout life, we have a need to feel safe and secure. We feel safest when we feel we are in control. We feel we are in control when we are in settings we recognize and understand, for that is where we are most secure in our knowledge and skills. We can use what we know in a repetitive and efficient way. We feel safe because we can control what will happen. Remember your experiences in sports, where the team members, much of the time, practiced fundamental routines until they felt secure in their abilities. We cannot perform very well if we have poor fundamentals or a weak knowledge.

Collaborate (upper left quadrant): We also need to feel nurtured and loved. We need to feel appreciated and cared for. We need to have meaningful relationships, to maintain profound contact. We need to cooperate and support one another. When we collaborate, we exercise our need to care for people and work together in trusting, cohesive relationships. In competition, a team wins by dominating its opponent. It can do this only if there is a high level of cooperation, teamwork, or cohesion among the separate team members.

Create (upper right quadrant): Finally, we have a need for stimulation, development, and growth. A living system is a growing system. To avoid stagnation and death, a system must be growing and developing. This means we have to change. But here's the challenge: change means moving outside our comfort zone and becoming something new. This process of learning and growing is associated with the capacity to do new things, to innovate and create. Think about this in terms of your sports experiences. Great performance always has an adaptive-creative element. We speak of taking over the momentum of a game. That means that our team has analyzed the other team's strategy and performance and has creatively adapted to it. We have innovated, and the other team cannot adapt to our new pattern.

At the individual level, each quadrant represents a basic human need. Some people feel some needs more than others. We don't all see life through the same lens, as it were. This can lead to problems, of course. Consider the example of coaching. Many coaches become fixed on the "Compete" quadrant. You have certainly known such coaches. They become obsessed with winning. They want to dominate their opponents. They get fixed on this singular focus, and it becomes their style of working—they start dominating everyone. It doesn't matter who it is—the other team, their own players, and anyone else within earshot. Most people naturally resent that kind of treatment, so they find ways to resist and strike back. When people try to give the coach feedback, it does not work. The coach "knows" he or she is right. We watched Bobby Knight lose his job for this reason. Domination was his way of operating.

The opposite case is the coach who approaches life more from the "Collaborate" quadrant. This person is often very warm and caring. He or she gives the players lots of freedom to operate. Most players enjoy working with a coach like this. The danger is that a coach with this style of working can be too lenient. The team never develops the discipline it needs. We watched Steve Fisher, a wonderful man whom we both know and admire, lose his job because people felt he had lost control of his program. People who emphasize the collaborative view worry a great deal about becoming too harsh or too domineering.

Some people see life through the "Control" quadrant. They are very concerned about maintaining the status quo. They tend to be highly disciplined and detail-focused. They are usually good at maintaining routines. In coaching, such a person has a strategic orientation that is carefully worked out and deeply ingrained in the players. The team becomes a "well-oiled machine." The problem is that like a machine, the team is predictable. The opposing team gains the advantage because it essentially know what the players are going to do. In this situation, feedback and criticism do not change the behavior of the coaches because they "know" they are right.

Some people see life through the "Create" quadrant. They tend to be visionary. They see the big picture. They notice changing trends. They are very good at adapting. They tend to be spontaneous and like to improvise. The problem is that they are often not disciplined. They get bored easily. They do not like to spend time on details or on fundamentals. They get criticized for being sloppy, but they resist the criticism because they know they are right.

~

Why is this model important? It all ties in with differentiation and integration. We usually find that it is much easier to differentiate between contrasting ideas than to integrate contrasting ideas. We feel the need to keep our differentiated concepts separate. To bring them together might violate our need for safety, order, and predictability, and we don't want to do that. We would rather stay in our comfort zone. The prospect of integrating contrasting ideas or styles brings up all sorts of ambiguity, confusion, and conflict. There's a part of us that believes that chaos is inherently bad and that we must strive to avoid or control it.

One way to maintain control is to invent a world without conflict. We all do this on a regular basis. We impose what we value on the world without giving any room to opposing positive values. I remember your days as a Boy Scout. You may have been the most unwilling Eagle Scout in history, but I'd be willing to bet that you can still recite the Boy Scout Law: "A Scout is trustworthy, loyal, helpful, friendly, courteous, kind, obedient, cheerful, thrifty, brave, clean, and reverent."

That credo reads like the description of the ideal boy. But what would that ideal boy look like if we examined him in terms of the Wholonics framework?

Collaborate (relational)	Helpful, friendly, courteous, kind, cheerful
Create (visionary)	—
Control (dependable)	Trustworthy, loyal, obedient, thrifty, clean, reverent
Compete (powerful)	Brave

I suspect that the authors who wrote the Boy Scout Law felt they had generated a list of wide scope. But that's not the case. While the Scout is valued for being dependable and relational, he is not very valued for being competitive and powerful. And there appears to be no value placed on the creative and visionary person, the one who sees things differently and who seeks to explore unknown paths. A cynic might say the ideal Scout is one who cheerfully stays within the boxes defined by adult authority. It makes me wonder what it would be like to be a Scout if the credo read, "A Scout is creative, independent, powerful, self-determining, challenging, strong, questioning, realistic, expansive, wise, engaged, and exuberant."

I hope this doesn't sound like an analytical game, because the implications are very real. For example, think of a boy living in a severely impoverished area. He might instinctively know that his very survival depends not on compliance to authority but on the values in the two right quadrants, "Compete" and "Create."

I don't mean to put down the Boy Scout movement. I think it has made great contributions. I am just using the Scout Law as a prominent illustration. In analyzing the Scout Law, I am illustrating something that *we all* do when we attempt to articulate the desired future. We all tend to articulate values that reflect unstated assumptions. Recently a woman was interviewed on a radio show. She had written a book based on the Bible that articulated the values she believed parents should use to raise children. All of the values fell in the lower left quadrant, "Control." Another author, also using the Bible as a source, could have articulated values in other quadrants. The problem was not in the Bible but in the person interpreting it. She had some very unconscious but powerful biases in her definition of what made a child "good." We might find what she did offensive and thus with indignation ask, How could she do that? The answer is, Pause and remember that we are this woman. We all do this. We interpret what is good by looking through that implicit lens that we ourselves most value. We may value the opposite quadrant and articulate very different values, but we are simply doing the same thing she is doing.

Wholonics can help us bring to the surface things that we may be missing. We can look at ourselves or look at an organization and ask, "Which quadrants are not represented, and what are the implications?"

In real life, we usually get very aggressive about arguing and defending the values we like or understand while just as aggressively rejecting anything that doesn't fit into the quadrants that allow us to stay in our comfort zone. In the process of acting with intention, we have to make arguments for what we believe is the best way to achieve our desired goals. So a manager who values order and control may say, "We don't want any loose cannons around here." He is implicitly saying, "We do not want anyone to take any initiative." Without realizing it, that manager is rejecting empowered action and change. The reverse is also possible, of course. The manager could reject order and deify change by saying something like, "We can no longer afford to have bureaucrats around here." By making this statement, the manager implicitly condemns control, order, and predictability.

Now, if you want to impress your friends, let me give you a big word that Gregory Bateson invented: *schismogenesis*. It means the creation of schisms and refers to arguments, theories, or perspectives that are broken or split (*schismo-*) at the outset (*genesis*). In almost every argument, one value is differentiated and chosen over its positive opposite. For example, "We must think of the good of my baby" or "We must think of the good of my career." While this may be a normal and even useful process, it has a downside in that it usually blinds us to the value of the positive opposite and leads us to a kind of success that will eventually turn into failure. We plant the seeds of failure at the outset of our problem-solving and planning processes.

Bateson was not the first to discover this phenomenon. The ancient Chinese sage Chuang Tzu understood it clearly. He pointed out that when we put too much emphasis on certain attributes to the exclusion of others, we get out of balance. Our thoughts get locked into rigid patterns, and we become stale and stressed. Chuang Tzu advocates a state of harmony in which opposites are blended. Here's an interpretation of him by Needleman and Appelbaum that I particularly like:

> As soon as the mind attaches itself to a single element ("this is good"), so implicitly or explicitly rejecting the opposing one ("this is bad"), we lose our finely poised integrity. The greater our reliance on such partial judgment, the more isolated we become from our own nature and the more we allow ourselves to exploit the rest of the natural world.

Chuang Tzu believed that to create balance, we must allow opposing ideas to work simultaneously, what he calls "taking both sides at once." In essence he is saying that we create more value when we consider and integrate positive oppositions. Many people have examined this logic and concluded that what the world needs is balance or compromise. But is that the answer? Not exactly, because people interpret this as an argument for self-compromise. Self-compromise always leads to failure. It is what occurs when we stay inside our comfort zones. We move into a state of entropy.

Through purpose-finding we leave our comfort zones and gain our sense of passion. The lesson is a powerful one: we are balanced not because we have compromised but because we have made a deep commitment to a purpose that we value. When we pursue purpose, we want to know what is real. We want feedback, even if it is negative. We want feedback even if it is from a quadrant we do not normally value. We are balanced because we are moving somewhere, open to all possible inputs as we reach out to learn new skills and new knowledge to get where we want to go. Once Shauri clarified her purpose, her definition of her relationship with Matt changed radically. She was living by a more powerful and more accurate view of reality and sense of purpose.

Shauri made a being change because she made a decision to be her best self. When Shauri clarified her purpose, she made fundamental decisions and came alive. She was filled with passion, gaining a more differentiated and more integrated self. She was more differentiated because she was taking all four quadrants into consideration, and she was more integrated because she was moving toward a higher purpose and that process was integrating the competing values.

I just now thought of another friend who looked at the Wholonics model and said, "I have big ideas. I am strong in the 'Create' quadrant, but I never pay attention to the details in the 'Control' quadrant." I challenged him and said, "I disagree.

You love to write music. I'll bet that when you are creating your music, you pay great attention to details."

He looked shocked. After a moment he said, "That's true!" He thought about it some more and asked me how I knew this.

The answer is that when we are fulfilling our core purposes, when we are doing the things we love, we are in dynamic balance. We have integrated the differences in the Wholonics model. When you are running a fast break, Garrett, you are creating even while you remain under control. You have an intense task focus while you stay connected and responsive to everyone on your team. You are both differentiated and integrated. You become enthusiastic about the creation of the future because you are creating it as you go.

Do you see what I am telling you—that you already know the fundamental elements of mastery? You have experienced them in sports and elsewhere.

By seeing things only through the lens of a particular set of values, we tend to get into a negative zone. What I'm suggesting is that any positive value, split from its positive opposite and pursued aggressively, will eventually create a negative outcome. In an organization, for example, the relational values in the "Collaborate" quadrant, pursued without the values of the opposite quadrant, will result in an organization that resembles a country club rather than a place of work. In fact, when I'm working with organizations, I call this the "irresponsible country club" pattern (see the accompanying figure). When we are applying the same principle to individuals, we see that the caring coach or leader becomes lax and lenient. Emphasize the quadrant directly opposite the "Collaborate" quadrant, and we produce the "oppressive sweatshop," where managers become tyrants and coaches become arrogant and domineering. At the individual level, the creative, visionary coach becomes a mere dreamer.

The Wholonics Model of Organizational Values.

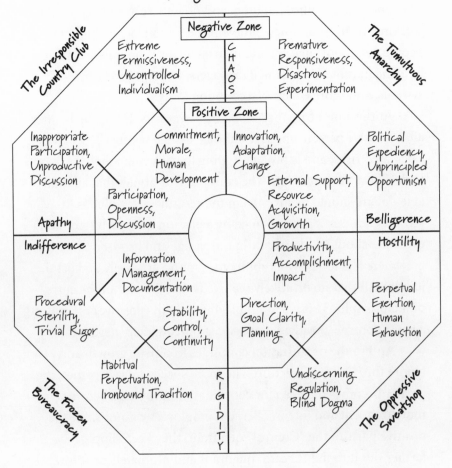

It's all too easy to get into the negative zone and sometimes not even realize it. In business the classic example is the entrepreneur, who is usually creative and willing to take risks. This person may invent some gadget and then put together a company. Soon there are eight people working in a dimly lit garage. The people are filled with hope and enthusiasm. They work well together, and they work hard. Their primary goal is to grow the company, and they are most creative in their efforts.

If they are successful at this stage, there is usually a big jump. They move to an office building, and now there are eighty people working. At this point new problems begin to emerge. Eighty people need coordination and management. Proposals are made to bring in more professional managers, better information systems, and more effective accounting tools.

At this point the entrepreneur often resists. He or she is, after all, a creative person who is usually excited by taking risks, at least calculated risks, and is probably going to condemn anything that looks like a "bureaucracy." The entrepreneur argues that all available dollars should be invested in the central goal, which is to grow. Often this is accompanied by a passionate speech reminding everyone about the days back in the garage and how the company got where it is today by its ability to respond creatively and get the job done. What no one likely realizes is that the plea of the entrepreneur is split. This person is playing growth (positive) off, not against control (positive), but against bureaucracy (negative).

And so the organization continues to pursue growth and ignore the need for structure. The more successful it becomes, the greater becomes the need for coordination. Problems become more frequent and intense. Because employees cannot value the positive parts of the "Control" quadrant, they keep slipping farther out into the "Create" quadrant and ultimately drift toward tumultuous anarchy. At this point they are producing less and less value.

Often at this point the entrepreneur—the founder, the parent figure—loses his or her job, fired by the board of directors. It seems inconceivable. Lots of people who are organizers then get hired. The creative people begin leaving. The new leaders save the company. Value increases. As they celebrate, they say, "No more of that creative crap around here." But all too soon the organization gets stale and begins to slip to the outer edges of the "Control" quadrant. There is less capacity to adapt to the changing preferences of the customer. In fact, the customer has become the enemy. The company begins to create less and less value. If it survives at all, there is another revolution within. And so the cycle goes, on and on.

Everyone in the foregoing scenario tends to believe that his or her situation is unique. The entire process is often explained in terms of personalities. Everyone is angry about the mean-spirited "politics" that have occurred. If these people were to read these paragraphs, they would be shocked to realize that someone unassociated with their situation could describe it so closely. Yet what is actually happening is totally predictable. They are playing out a cycle that has gone on many times before. They cannot see it because they do not have the advantage of the Wholonics model.

Remember my mentioning the firings of Bobby Knight and Steve Fisher? One was accused of being overbearing and rigid (too far into the "Compete" and "Control" quadrants). The other was accused of being too lenient and having no control of his program (too far into the "Collaborate" quadrant). Though we'd probably rather not see it, you and I do similar things. We enter the negative zone because we are not naturally talented at differentiating and integrating effectively. When the success of one set of values calls forth the need for the opposite positive values, we see only conflict. I think this stimulates the fight-or-flight response, which is as ancient as life itself. We cannot imagine how to embrace the oppositions and allow the energy in the seeming conflict propel us to a higher level of capacity. If we are to get beyond this and open ourselves up to the integration of the positive opposites, we must abandon our problem-solving mode and ask the key question, "What result do I want to create?"

The purpose of Wholonics reasoning—locating and integrating positive opposites—is to help people consciously increase their complexity, to make them more effective, to help them live in a creative rather than a reactive state. Normal thinking does not take both sides at once. Normal discourse makes it almost impossible to see and integrate positive opposites. So we vacillate. We pursue any given value until it becomes counterproductive and only then—if we are lucky—do we pursue its positive opposite.

In going back and forth, we get trapped into perpetual problem-solving. We live in a reactive mode. In the reactive mode we tend to become self-focused. In this process we greatly differentiate the self from the environment and the people in the environment. We tend to lose almost all sense of integration with our world. We tend to act *on* the environment, not *with* it. We do not join in the cocreation of a higher purpose. We impose our will: "Well, I'm taking the job in Cairo whether you like it or not!" Here the value is on compliance and not on a healthy relationship or the cocreation of a commonly desired result.

When we differentiate ourselves from the tension or the resistance to our intent, we do not recognize that we are part of the pattern in question, that we are still integrated with it. Purpose becomes more important than process and relationship. We do not recognize the feedback loops that emerge when we simply demand compliance. We are blinded to the fact that we may be destroying the relationship and a precious part of ourselves. The more we deceive ourselves into believing we are not integrated with that on which we act, the more dangerous we become. We destroy the environment while not seeing that we are an integral part of it. We do not see that in destroying that environment, we are destroying ourselves. We engage in patterns of evil.

I don't know if I shared this story with you or not, but last year, on a spring day, I was in the backyard watching the geese and ducks swim around the pond. There were several new mother ducks. They were proudly leading their little ones in tight formations as they moved about. There was also a male swan swimming close by. Since his mate had starting nesting, he had been most assertive in his territorial claims. Lately, however, he had been more docile, and I was not prepared for what happened next.

A mother and her ducklings were passing when, like summer lightning, the swan suddenly thrust himself into the formation. There was chaos, and then, in an instant, the mother had all but one of the ducklings gathered. The swan moved between the lone duckling and its mother. Each time the duckling would try to move toward the mother, the swan would cut it off and drive it closer to shore. The mother tried to attack the swan, but she could not distract it. I yelled at the swan and looked for something to throw. The terrified duckling dived under the water. The long neck of the swan followed it under and grasped it in its mouth. It crushed the duckling and spit it out. The swan then swam off. The disoriented mother duck circled the dead baby. After a few moments, she returned to the needs of her remaining offspring.

I was greatly affected by this event. For three days I reacted emotionally to the swan's violent act. That act seemed to represent everything bad that could happen in the world. I thought about the nightly news and the terrible things that people inflict on one another. I thought about my professional work and the armies of brilliant but disempowered executives who vie for resources while living lives of fear. What do they fear? They fear the organizational swans, the bigger, more powerful birds that will eat their ducklings (or them). They explain that organizational life is a Darwinian competition and it's easy to get eaten. It's nice to pretend that we can trust, but the real secret is to always be in control. In order to survive, you have to be a good technical problem solver and a very clever politician. Or so it would seem!

In this normal worldview there are some core assumptions about what is good and how we should behave. Good is survival.

We need to survive. In pursuing survival we also tend to flee pain and seek pleasure. We also seek to obtain power and maintain control. Life is a basic exercise in politicoeconomic transaction. It is a competition for resources, and as the bumper sticker says, "He who dies with the most toys wins."

The reason I was upset with the events on the pond is that my entire professional life is dedicated to helping people move beyond such dire assumptions as those I've just described. I have spent three decades trying to learn how to help people move from being externally driven and self-focused to being internally driven and other-focused. I have tried to learn how to move people from the natural choice of personal good over collective good to the integration of personal good and collective good. But this is not easy. The Darwinian worldview is based on fact. After all, duck-lings do get eaten. Yet the worldview itself, unconnected to its positive opposite, is more dangerous than the swans that are so feared.

I personally embrace the Darwinian worldview all the time. When I do, I become like the people I am describing. I become filled with fear. I become reactive and lose meaning. I behave in ways that produce negative emotions. At such times I tend to completely lose my best self. I strive to preserve old realities, and I feel the encompassing boundaries of slow death closing in on me. I am not moving and growing. I become increasingly less secure and more externally driven. I become less caring and more self-focused. My past and my future are not integrated, and I can no longer understand the story that I am. I am lost, alienated. While I know I need to take action, taking action is impossible. I get depressed.

What's worse, and more dangerous, is that when I enter this dark state, I tend to deny that it is happening. The denial allows me to avoid accountability. It allows me to continue to wallow in my self-pity and my rationalizations. At such times I need to move from slow death to deep change, yet the idea of finding purpose and making change seems impossible.

At these times my strategies become particularly split. I can get completely out of touch with the paradoxical truth that change cannot happen unless there is stability, and stability cannot exist unless there is change. Strategically, we cannot change ourselves unless we become more stable—but stable in a very particular and very dynamic way. That is what purpose-finding does for us. It creates a point of stability from which we can allow other aspects of ourselves to change and come into alignment with our more valued point of stability.

When we clarify our values and find our purpose, we make a change in our being state. We find a center, a point of stability. That sense of increased order and purpose is what allows us to take risks, to act within the face of uncertainty. As soon as we make such movement, we feel increased integrity. Our past and present again connect. We understand the story that we are. We have a new self that is aligned with emergent reality. Our awareness expands. We feel empowered. We become empowering to others. Instead of acting *on* our environment, we act *with* our environment. We cocreate, and new resources flow. At that moment, we leave normal reasoning and normal intent. At that moment, we begin to enact our best self. When our best self is in action, we become filled with positive emotions.

Because we are now different, we see differently. We see ourselves in a world of abundant resources. In pursuing our purpose, we stop reacting and start making choices. We often choose to reverse that natural assumption by fleeing pleasure instead of pain and embracing pain instead of pleasure. Toys may lose their importance. Indeed, we come to recognize that survival is not the first law of nature. The first law of nature is that the universe seeks to evolve to a higher level of complexity. To facilitate that evolution is to make a profound contribution. At that point of increased awareness, we may even become willing to violate the central assumption of personal survival.

The truth is that there are swans on the pond of life, and they may eat our babies. The technicopolitical world is a dangerous place. All that is real, and it can and does lead us to a life of fear. Yet it is also possible to enter a reality that accepts but transcends the technicopolitical reality. When we enter that higher being state, we come to a stunning new definition of evil and of good. There's a wonderful statement by a psychologist that I'm fond of quoting, Mihalyi Csikszentmihalyi:

> Entropy or evil is the default state, the condition to which systems return unless work is done to prevent it. What prevents it is what we call "good"—actions that preserve order while preventing rigidity, that are informed by the needs of the most evolved systems. Acts that take into account the future, the common good, the emotional well-being of others. Good is the creative overcoming of inertia, the energy that leads to the evolution of human consciousness. To act in terms of new principles of organization is always more difficult, and requires more effort and energy. The ability to do so is what has been known as virtue.

Csikszentmihalyi's insights here are important, particularly the concept that the default state in life is entropy or slow death. Entropy happens to every system that is not working to prevent its own stagnation and death. It happens to you and it happens to me. It happens to groups and organizations. It happens to every system in nature. The thing that prevents entropy or slow death is action, a special kind of action. Indeed, this action is the very thing we call "good."

By now it should be clear that this special kind of action is at the heart of profound contact. It is a key Wholonics concept. It is action that "preserves order while preventing rigidity"—action that allows us to integrate differentiated concepts of stability and change. Good is action that preserves order while simultaneously fostering and supporting change. It is action that is "informed by the needs of the most evolved systems." So the order we are preserving and the changes we are making contribute value to the systems around us that are also changing in a similar manner.

When we are involved in "good action," we are not problem-solving. We are, by choice, creators. Our commitment keeps us integrated despite the fear and pain that change involves. This kind of action challenges us to bring forth our best self. When the best self unfolds in this way, we become more inner-directed and other-focused. We enter a more connected state, an awareness of the "future, the common good, the emotional well-being of others." That is, when we make deep personal change, we create a more integrated set of relationships, a more empowered community that benefits others and benefits us. We integrate with this new set of relationships while letting go of some older set of relationships.

Good is "the creative overcoming of inertia, the energy that leads to the evolution of human consciousness," allowing us to see reality in a new way. We model higher levels of courage and integrity and thus attract others to empowerment and integration. And so we return again to the idea that *we lead change by being change.*

To become integrated with the best me, I change both me and you. By making a being change, I act "in terms of new principles of organization." I move to a higher level of reality and morality. Instead of allowing entropy, I engage in the reinvention of self, and I become the stimulus of a new and higher order, the unfolding of the potential that now exists. We now begin moving swiftly from old principles of organizing to the new principles of organizing. That is your challenge—to move forward by clarifying purpose, exercising courage, and ever becoming a new person, your best self. I am not sure that any of us ever do this alone. Sometimes we need help, and that is fine. The key is to be in the process of becoming. When we are, we expand in mastery and find joy in life.

Love,

Dad

Practice Responsible Freedom

Dear Garrett,

Thank you for your last letter. The first thing that jumped off the page at me was this:

> *I am often in the negative zone. Some may even say that I created the negative zone. You were right about me having trouble with letting go of my past lifestyle. I was very happy with where I was and what I was about. It's hard for anyone going through a major change in life. I feel like it has been especially hard for me.*

The truth is that we are all like you. We all enter the negative zone. When you say you feel like you created the negative zone, you are right, at a deeper level than you might realize. You did create it. We all create it for ourselves. The only way we can get into the negative zone is if we create it. Now, we do not do it alone. Our circumstances and relationships contribute to it. We interact with our circumstances and our relationships in such a way as to create the reality that we live in. So the more accurate statement is this, you *cocreated* the negative zone.

You also talked about letting go of your "past lifestyle." That makes a lot of sense to me, in that very few people live as happily as you did in high school. You were an initiator, a leader, and a master. You were the person that lifted others out of their negative zones. To leave high school and home was a major life change, and it was not easy. None of us should be surprised that you might be feeling depressed after changes like this.

I think it's important to realize that you are not alone, that similar things happen to millions of people. At such times it is normal to fall into negative routines that lead toward increased entropy or slow death. Alcohol, drugs, smoking, overeating, sleep, money, power, status, sex, pornography, gambling, and procrastination are just a few of the things around which negative routines can center. Such routines can lead away from vitality and toward destruction of the best self. We get depressed and lose hope. Sometimes we cannot even imagine experiencing a life centered around the actualization of the best self. Here is a personal story, written by a psychologist named James Prochaska, that I think you will find very interesting. He describes the feelings and experiences of depression. As he graduated from high school, he began to experience a number of negative emotions.

At the time I was convinced that everything would be downhill from then on, and I became anxious, depressed, and cynical. When I finally overcame my psychological distress, I felt fortunate that I had not given up on life.

However, I did not learn my lesson well enough. After graduating from college, I chose a graduate school that turned out to be the wrong one for me. My feelings of despair returned. I began drinking too much, eating too much, and sleeping too much. I was training to become a clinical psychologist and became nervous that my peers and professors would find out about my behavior. So I closed myself off from outside help, which made me even more distressed and demoralized.

Fortunately, I was able to enroll in a university located near my friends and family. When I finally overcame this second period of distress, I felt foolish for not having learned

more from the first episode. Only after three or four times of
experiencing life as peaking and passing me by did I finally
learn that life only passes you by when you give up on your
abilities to change.

One of the most poignant parts of this story is the emotional
distress he experiences because of his fear that life would be all
downhill after high school. Fear can paralyze us. We stop looking
to the future in a positive way. We do not see it as a good thing
that it is our responsibility to create. His fears put him in the
reactive mode and into a life of problems. And it is then that he
moves into a life of anxiety, depression, and cynicism. This is such
a common pattern that I think everyone has experienced it at
some time and to some extent.

Prochaska is eventually able to pull out of his depression.
Nevertheless, he later finds himself in another difficult situation,
and the pattern returns. This time he calls on alcohol, food, and
sleep to escape. The problem with these common escape mechanisms is that they make us less able than ever to pursue purpose
and thus experience our best selves. This is what happened to him.
He was less and less able to pursue a degree. The fear of being
discovered led him to withdraw from the help that might have
been available to him, until he was cut off from others. This loss
of social support reinforced all of his bad habits. He grew further
distressed and demoralized.

I can't help but think about your situation, how you left a
network of rich, supportive relationships. You arrived in college
and found yourself living with a randomly selected set of roommates. You describe the situation as truly terrible. Our social settings are critical. It is through our interactions with them that we
cocreate the reality we live in. I often emphasize to college students
that they need to take control of their living situation. They need

to consider the kinds of roommates they have and ask, What result do I want to create? How do I want to live? We need to create a social context that supports our growth. Many college students never grasp the importance of taking control of this variable. What's worse, many people go through their entire lives without controlling their living situation. I am glad you say that when you think back on your first-semester living arrangements, you get angry. I hope those strong feelings lead you to a future in which you always control your social context and your living arrangements.

Eventually Prochaska works himself out of his first difficulty but then goes through two more episodes just like it. He says he felt foolish for not learning from the first experience, yet he still repeated the pattern. Finally he does learn. At that point he says, *"Life only passes you by when you give up on your abilities to change."* I love that sentence. It is critical that we never give up on developing and maintaining our abilities to change. That is why overcoming negative routines and maintaining positive ones is so important.

Becoming one's best self means always changing and growing. This means learning how to transcend the polarities of life. Like most people, I often get trapped in the negative zone. I end up stagnating. There is a paradox about change. To be able to change, we need to become more stable, but being stable does not mean being stagnant. We stabilize ourselves at one level so that we can change ourselves at another, and so, in an ideal world, we become simultaneously stable and adaptive. We need to find the elusive middle ground that integrates positive opposites.

This is where the role of routines comes into play. By its nature, a routine is an activity or practice that has become regimented or internalized. As I was thinking about this just now, I remembered a good example. Do you remember in basketball when your coach insisted that you regularly work out in the weight room? That was a routine that helped you grow in terms of muscular capacity. As you stabilized that routine in your life, you kept increasing in that capacity. That increased capacity made you more adaptive on the basketball court. Because you were stronger, you had more things you could do and more choices you could make. Ultimately, then, this positive routine increased your freedom.

Often when I start feeling depressed, it is associated with a feeling of losing meaning in my life. I also find at these times that I have slipped out of some positive routines that are important to me. At such times I evaluate myself and give myself a report card on how I am doing in terms of my life statement. Here's one of the first things I look at: my "daily life strategy checklist" as I've recorded it in my life statement:

> *To accomplish these things, I am exercising, controlling diet, evolving physically, studying, praying, closing integrity gaps, experiencing inspiration, tending to family, tending to others, saving mornings for creative demands, controlling commitments, focusing professionally, disciplining finances, and playing.*

The overall daily life strategy checklist allows me to quickly determine whether I have all my routines in place. If I do, I am likely to be stable and adaptive. If I find I've slipped in some of my routines, I go back and make a course correction, reconnecting with the disciplines I've been neglecting. I confess that there are times when I get more deeply stuck and my checklist is not enough. It is as if I get trapped in some cage—usually called *negative routines, addictions,* or *self-defeating behaviors.*

At those times in our lives when we slip into negative routines, it is possible to step back and come to a deeper understanding of the difference between being in the reactive state and being in the extraordinary state. You can make that first step back by moving from problem-solving to purpose-finding. The trouble is that in our efforts to dull the pain of feeling trapped, we turn to the types of addictions I listed above—alcohol, drugs, smoking, overeating, sleep, money, power, status, sex, pornography, gambling, and procrastination. These become demons ruling our lives, and we surrender our freedom to them, literally becoming their slaves. Needless to say, that's when we start feeling hopeless. We have reduced self-control. Yet all is not lost. Even in the depths of hopelessness, we can change.

James Prochaska, the man who wrote the story about his depression, and two other scholars, John Norcross and Carlo DiClemente, executed a research program at the University of Rhode Island. He and the others spent years studying what people do to pull out of negative routines and addictions. They found that all change is self-change, even if someone is seeing a professional, because ultimately it is our own decision to change that sets the change in motion. The insights that come from this research are very useful. Let's take a look at some of the high points.

When interviewed, most people who have made successful self-changes describe the process in pretty simplistic terms. They may say, for example, that they woke up one morning and just decided to do it. They believe what they are saying, but much more is actually involved. The researchers found that these people actually tend to go through six stages: precontemplation, contemplation, preparation, action, maintenance, and termination. Everyone has to go through these stages. Someone who is depressed must go through them. Someone who wants to quit smoking or who wants to lose weight must go through them. This six-stage process is pretty much universal.

Part of the reason we tend not to see the six stages is that most of us equate change with action. But it's important to keep in mind that even while we are moving toward change, we are in *nonaction* stages 80 percent of the time. To successfully make self-change, it is important to know which stage we are in at any given moment. Each stage is characterized by different change strategies. If we try to use strategies that don't belong with the stage we are presently in, we are setting ourselves up to fail. The strategies are listed in the accompanying table. Here's an outline of how the stages work:

Precontemplation. In this stage we have a problem but don't yet see it as a problem. Every one of us is perpetually in this stage in regard to at least some of our negative routines or self-defeating behaviors. Other people may see our problem clearly, but we do not. In this stage we have no intention of changing our behavior. For example, a man comes home from work every night, eats, watches television, and falls asleep. He has no interest in anything, including family members and visitors. In the precontemplation stage, he does not see that his behavior is causing problems for other people. He denies any suggestion that he might have a problem. If he perceives any need for change, it is only that he would like people to stop criticizing him.

Resistance and denial are the bywords of this stage. If a person ends up in therapy at this point, it is only due to pressure from the boss, a spouse, a peer—in short, somebody who has leveraged them into going. In therapy they are noncooperative and usually stop going as soon as they can reasonably do so. In your last letter you reflected that "as far as the psychologist goes, I didn't give him much of a chance. I was just waiting for him to do something I didn't like so I could stop going." That's a pretty standard precontemplation response.

Summary of Some Change Process Techniques.

Process	Goals	Techniques[a]
Consciousness-Raising	Increasing information about self and problem	Observations, confrontations, interpretations, bibliotherapy
Social Liberation	Increasing social alternatives for behaviors that are not problematic	Advocating for rights of repressed, empowering, policy interventions
Emotional Arousal	Experiencing and expressing feelings about one's problems and solutions	Psychodrama, grieving losses, role playing
Self-Reevaluation	Assessing feelings and thoughts about self with respect to a problem	Value clarification, imagery, corrective emotional experience
Commitment	Choosing and committing to act, or belief in ability to change	Decision-making therapy, New Year's resolutions, logotherapy
Countering	Substituting alternatives for problem behaviors	Relaxation, desensitization, assertion, positive self-statements
Environment Control	Avoiding stimuli that elicit problem behaviors	Environmental restructuring (e.g., removing alcohol or fattening foods), avoiding high-risk cues
Reward	Rewarding self, or being rewarded by others, for making changes	Contingency contracts, overt and covert reinforcement
Helping Relationships	Enlisting the help of someone who cares	Therapeutic alliance, social support, self-help groups

[a]These are primarily professional techniques used by psychotherapists.

Source: Prochaska, Norcross, and DiClemente,1994, p. 33. Used with permission.

Interestingly, while we are in the precontemplation stage, we often feel demoralized. Why? Because we see our problem as hopeless. No wonder we go into denial about it! We give in to our hopelessness, and the problem grows in magnitude until we feel like we are being stalked by a hulking monster. On the bright side, we now know that it helps people just to know that this feeling of demoralization is characteristic of this stage and that regardless of how we might feel, it is possible to change. This knowledge thus becomes a potential source of hope.

Some people believe that reaching people in this stage is impossible. They argue that the best thing to do is to wait until the person with the problem hits bottom, when he or she will be more willing to receive outside help. The trouble is that the problem can snowball, making it increasingly difficult for the person to change. We need to try to help people in this stage, even when it can be discouraging for us. It usually requires us to make a being change so that we can lead change.

At this stage only two strategies seem to be useful: consciousness-raising (getting more information about the problem) and social liberation (finding positive social situations). The discussions between you and me have, I hope, served as consciousness-raising, and your association with a more positive group of people has been socially liberating. It's my observation that in the late fall you were just beginning to leave the precontemplation stage. You were beginning to accept the idea that perhaps you were depressed.

Contemplation. I recognize that I'm moving into the contemplation stage when I start thinking about taking action. I've begun to want to change how I feel about myself. I open up to new information, though I'm not yet ready to act. You might say that I know the end result I want and may even know the path I plan to take, but I'm not ready to leave on the trip. In the book by Prochaska and his colleagues, I found it interesting that smokers spend about two years in the contemplation stage. The fear of failure is a big factor, accounting for endless excuses and procrastination. I also found it interesting that the clearest sign of moving out of this stage is the movement away from problem-solving and toward focusing on solutions. That certainly aligns with my own experience, where I become focused on the future instead of the past.

Four coping strategies are effective here: consciousness-raising, social liberation, emotional arousal, and self-evaluation. Emotional arousal means moving from thinking to feeling, experiencing and expressing feelings about the problem. Self-reevaluation means analyzing the feelings and thoughts about oneself in relation to the problem.

You went into this stage when you started expressing a desire to feel differently. You became more interested in discussing information about depression. This fact is reflected in many of the letters you have written. You were contemplating change, but you were still not prepared to act. To your credit, you eventually moved on.

Preparation. This is an interesting stage. It's at this point that people are planning to take action within a month. This stage is characterized by commitment and readiness but also great ambivalence. For my own part, at this stage I find myself going through the final preparations to begin the journey. I have already made some changes. I've stopped denying, have gathered some information, and usually have cut back to some degree on the problem behavior. Yet I am not quite ready. This stage is an important step in the process of getting ready.

Consciousness-raising has by now fallen away as a coping mechanism. Social liberation, emotional arousal, and self-reevaluation are still effective. The additional effective coping mechanism is commitment. Commitment means believing in one's ability to change and making the choice to act.

Action. I know I'm in this stage when I start engaging in new patterns of behavior. Obvious examples are when a smoker throws all his or her cigarettes away or an alcoholic dumps all the alcohol down the drain. Since these patterns are visible, other people finally see some change taking place and start giving encouragement and support. Standing outside the action as an objective observer, it's difficult to understand that the change started before this stage or that more will continue after it. Understanding this, I've certainly seen more clearly how important it can be to get support in the earlier and later stages.

You may have recognized that in the past two weeks you have entered this stage. You began with seeing the doctor and following his advice. That was a huge step forward. Your sister saw you taking this action. She got excited and paid greater attention. She let you know that she saw a difference, and she shared her excitement with you. You, in turn, started to show a more positive orientation. Recall that in an earlier letter you expressed an entirely different attitude toward therapy: you were looking for a reason to drop it and saw the psychologist's behavior as the problem. Now you are expressing a commitment to doing better with a new psychologist when you get home in a couple of weeks.

I respond positively to your new behavior, just as your sister did. I rejoice in your sense of progress. Yet in fact you were changing all along. It is just difficult for observers to realize that because they do not understand that the stages before action are also part of the change process.

In the action stage, information and self-evaluation become less important than social liberation and commitment. Four additional processes also become relevant at this point: reward, countering, control of the environment, and helping relationships.

Reward simply means setting up ways to acknowledge your accomplishments. These could come from yourself or others—

ideally both. You might, for example, identify some touchstones of progress and promise yourself a positive reward as you reach each objective. For instance, people on diets sometimes promise themselves new wardrobes when they attain a certain weight.

Countering means replacing a negative behavior with a positive one. For instance, a person who is giving up smoking may substitute chewing gum for cigarettes. What works best for me is to make a list of behaviors that I feel are self-defeating for me and then identify positive routines that might replace them. You might substitute a rigorous training program for a pattern of sleeping late.

Environmental control means that we make sure we are spending our time in situations where our problem behaviors are not encouraged and where our positive behaviors are valued. An alcoholic, for example, would avoid places where people are drinking.

You yourself put environmental control into action when you decided to move out of the living situation you were in at school. And you employed it when you started spending your time with more positive people. And when you are at home, you are spending time with people who provide opportunities for positive behavior. At this stage we are looking for contexts that would help us cocreate our best self.

Helping Relationships. This stage involves asking for support from people who care by talking openly about feeling depressed and discussing any negative routines you might have. It is asking people to help you do things that call forth your best self. People tend to be very responsive to such requests.

Maintenance. Change does not stop just because you've taken action. Afterward comes the maintenance stage. This is when we consolidate the progress made in all the earlier stages. We put energy into guarding against relapses. Remember the story Prochaska told. He got depressed by leaving high school and worked his way out of it. Yet he did not learn enough to prevent it from happening again. He went through four bouts with depression before he was able to recognize the early symptoms and stay out of the negative zone. This stage may be short, or it may last a lifetime. In this stage commitment, reward, countering, environmental control, and helping relationships are the operative coping mechanisms.

Termination. In this stage the old behavior is no longer a temptation, for we have lost all desire for the negative pattern. We have confidence that we will not relapse. We have achieved victory over self. There seems to be great variation in the way different people handle this stage. One person may be able to completely conquer smoking and lose all desire. Others, even twenty years later, are still yearning for the old satisfactions. For such people it is necessary to stay in the maintenance stage. The same appears to be true for alcoholics and even dieters.

Being human, few of us move through this process in a straight line, stage one to stage two and so on to stage six. Prochaska and his associates found that this happens in only about 20 percent of cases. We might do well in some stages and poorly in others, thus following what might seem like a chaotic pattern through the different stages. Change often requires a great deal of energy, time, and money, and the truth is that most of us underestimate what's involved. So we might have many starts and stops, with the average person going through the entire process as many as six times!

About two months ago, you and I had a number of phone conversations. From one call to another I noticed a lot of variation in where you were. I would feel that you were making progress and were close to taking action. Then I would talk to you again and you seemed negative and further away from taking action. I would feel discouraged. Then I would remember this model and realize that you are actually engaged in a very positive process. Let me explain.

The people researching this process came to call their model the "spiral model of change" (see the accompanying figure). They see progress as a spiral on two axes, showing that we move forward

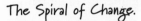

The Spiral of Change.

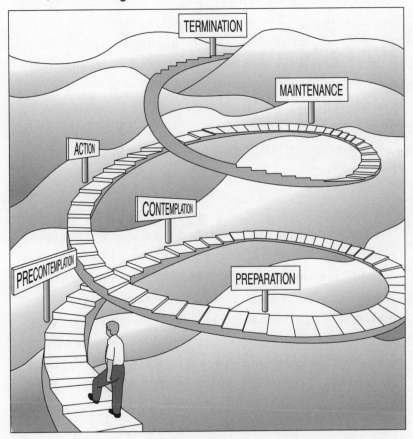

Source: Prochaska, Norcross, and DiClemente, 1994, p. 49. Used with permission.

and backward on the horizontal axis. The process seems discouraging, but there is a very positive fact that we often do not realize: this spiral process is also moving on a vertical axis, and we are continually moving upward toward success. Both our forward and backward movements are actually part of a larger learning process. I believe that this is what is happening to you.

Change is a messy process that includes failures. When faced with the failures, we feel frustration, shame, and other negative emotions. If we do not know that this is a natural part of the process, we may tend to collapse in discouragement and despair. If we realize that failure is part of progress, we can perhaps engage it more positively. By recycling, you are learning about yourself and developing an increased capacity for growth. Action followed by relapse is far better than taking no action at all because those who act and fail and keep on going are twice as likely to succeed in the next six months than people who have not yet acted. The lesson here is very clear: do not focus on the failure. Be like Rocky and keep getting up off the mat! As it says on a health poster, "Never quit quitting."

Negative patterns are related to one another. For example, the most frequent cause of relapse for smoking, drinking, and overeating is emotional distress. Therefore, a person might quit smoking but replace it with eating and then put on weight. Smokers who also drink are twice as likely to return to smoking. There are many such examples in everyday life. People give up one negative pattern but then adopt another to replace it. My advice is to consider all such patterns as ultimately being related, and if you want change to be permanent, you've got to understand the underlying causes of your distress. We need to look deeply into ourselves.

There's a popular misconception that the only reason we don't change is that we lack willpower or commitment. Commitment is one of the nine processes of change, but to rely only on commitment or willpower is to set oneself up for failure.

Balanced Vision. One of the change processes is called "self-reevaluation." It actually takes two forms: one focuses on the present and one on the future. The present form takes a negative view and primarily emphasizes our present bad characteristics and emotions. The future form envisions a changed, happier, and healthier self. The most effective evaluations contain both. The negative pushes us out of the present, while the positive pulls us into the future. I suspect that most people think about their problems and invite feedback on their problems. Few people think about the possible future or invite feedback on their best self. Again, we come back to the same key principle, that we need to move away from problem-solving toward purpose-finding. We need to be able to hold in our mind a compelling picture of a better future.

Anxiety. Change always involves uncertainty since there really are no absolute guarantees of success in life. It is therefore natural to practice avoidance. We put off starting as a way to protect ourselves from failure. Committing to change is never easy, but the research has revealed five pieces of advice that can help:

1. Plan to take small steps.
2. Set a specific starting date so that you neither act prematurely nor procrastinate.
3. Go public with your commitment so that you will be motivated by knowing that others are expecting you to succeed and so are more likely to help you get back on track if you have a relapse.
4. Prepare as if you were going in for major surgery. Since change is often the psychological equivalent of major

physical surgery, you and your support group should give this process a high priority.

5. Create your own action plan. By creating your own plan, you increase the likelihood that you will act.

Loss. One of the reasons it is difficult to maintain an important change that we've made is that most changes require us to give something up. If I am an alcoholic, my alcoholism may have destroyed my family and cost me my job. Even so, giving up alcohol means losing a crutch that I have trusted, perhaps for a very long time. To truly change, we need to go through the process of mourning. It is natural to miss our old habits and everything involved in them. For example, the alcoholic gives up going to a bar where he enjoyed some level of camaraderie with a familiar circle of people. I think that with your graduation from high school, you began to mourn the loss of many things you greatly valued.

Service. One of the things that helps in the maintenance stage is serving others. When you begin healing your psychological and spiritual wounds, you feel more whole, and your attention often turns to helping others. Doing so puts you into relationships of caring, compassion, and love. In these relationships everyone is healed, both those who give and those who receive. By focusing on service, we can accelerate our own healing process.

Social Networks. We live in groups or social networks. Our groups have norms, values, and roles. In any group we participate in, we are expected to be a certain way. Often when we are contemplating change, we worry about the resistance we will get from family members, peers, or others who are important to us. Fear of their reactions can keep you from taking action. If you do take action, you may relapse because of the reactions of the people around you and your desire to please them. It is important to consider this issue, and it may even be necessary to choose to move into a new network of supporters that will support your success in whatever you choose to do with your life.

Of all the insights that came out of the research by Prochaska and his associates, I have to say the one about freedom strikes me the most. It's shocking to learn that as otherwise intelligent human beings, we resist becoming aware of the problems that are endangering or destroying us. We seemingly prefer to suffer rather than give up control—or at least our illusion of control. Many of us seem to say, "No one is going to tell me what to do, no matter what the consequences!" The authors of the study call this orientation "foolish freedom" as opposed to "responsible freedom."

In your last letter to me you reflected on how difficult it can be to look at ourselves. You also noted how hardheaded you can be and what a challenge it is for you to look at your values and beliefs and discover they are off. You even commented about your resistance to accepting that somebody else might be right.

You may find this hard to believe, but you were describing not just yourself but all of us. Foolish freedom is an obsessive need for control. When we are caught up in that kind of thinking, it's as if we are saying that we must cling to our illusions of control at all costs. Often we get into this pattern as a reaction to our parents or some other overcontrolling authority figure. We rebel and vow that never again will we allow anyone to control us. We become fiercely and foolishly independent. Some people carry this pattern through their entire adult lives.

We develop routines to ensure that we cannot be controlled. For example, procrastination and withdrawal are ways that we can exert control over other people. Every time someone pressures us to make a responsible decision, no matter how simple or serious, we simply withdraw. Someone says, "If you want to go to watch the play with me, you will have to decide because I must order the tickets." You reply, "OK, just forget it. I'm not going to go." By

procrastinating and withdrawing, people pass by one positive experience after another. They lock onto the path of least resistance
and live a life trapped in their comfort zones. As they stagnate,
they cannot help but become depressed. Such foolish freedom is
not freedom at all but a self-imposed imprisonment.

Last year when you first started getting depressed, your mom
approached you with several decisions that would shape your
future: having the coach talk to recruiters, setting up opportunities
for you to talk to recruiters, sending in applications to schools,
deciding where to live and with whom, and many similar issues.
Each one required some degree of commitment in the face of
uncertainty and ambiguity. The natural thing to do was to procrastinate or withdraw—and that, of course, was the very natural
path of least resistance, which always leads toward entropy and
slow death. Foolish freedom is not freedom at all.

From a Wholonics perspective, the pattern of foolish freedom means we have embraced one positive value (freedom) and
cut off the positive opposition (responsibility). And so we move
into the negative zone, become defensive, and deny anything that
suggests that we need to change.

When we can move beyond a problem-solving pattern and
answer the question "What result do I want to create?" we can
move toward the creation of our desired result, a place where we
can express our newest and best self. And that's where we find true
freedom! We find increased strength and develop greater resolve.
We more easily leave our problems behind. As we move toward
purpose, we experience victory over self. We trade depression for
hope. We move forward with confidence as we create a better and
better world around us. As we create a better world, we create
a better self. We are then more open to learning about that self,
to increase our consciousness.

Foolish freedom is inherently reactive. Responsible freedom takes us into the extraordinary or creative being state. We become creators of our best selves. As Robert Fritz observes, creators create if they are having positive emotions, and they create if they are having negative emotions. Because they know where they must go, they are less influenced by emotions. They also hunger for accurate feedback, both positive and negative, because they feel they must be in touch with reality. Because they know what result they want to create, they proceed in creating it. They do not dread error and failure but embrace it and squeeze the learning out of it.

It is only in this creative state that we are responsible and free. It is then that we can be comfortable and open to receive help from others. Because we truly know who we are, we have no fear of manipulation and control. Indeed, it is then that we cannot be manipulated and controlled. When we live in the extraordinary being state, we are empowered and empowering.

In your case you have two pretty intense parents. We therefore get into control. Both your mom and I try hard to monitor and curb our impulses to control, but we often end up exerting control anyway. In addition, you have some pretty intense siblings. You have had to work hard to have a strong sense of self, but you have always seemed to be particularly clear about who you are. Since you seemed so clear, I did not worry so much about you in that respect. I think in this past year, control issues have really come to the fore. I have tried to minimize control, but I have sometimes failed. For example, when you called and asked about going to the clinic for basketball coaches in Las Vegas, I thought I asked some logical questions. The next day your mom said you were not going to go because you could not meet all the expectations and commitments I was expressing. I now know that you only wanted to go to the clinic to get additional information about coaching. The

information might help you make some decisions. You were not
ready to make any commitments about your future. When I learned
that you felt I had been pressuring you, I was stunned and wanted
to deny that I had done so. Instead I pushed my "defenses off"
button and tried to look at it from your point of view. Sure enough,
what I had perceived as "gentle questions" sure looked like "demands for control." You'd been exactly right! I felt terrible and I
apologize. I am not sure how long it will take for me to fully grow
up as a parent. In fact, I may still be in the resistant, precontemplation stage of my growth around that one.

That said, I want to move away from discussing negative
patterns and focus more on how we practice responsible freedom.
For me, this begins with monitoring my behavior in terms of the
positive routines that give me energy. A positive routine is regimented practice that stabilizes us so that we can continue to grow.
Working out in the weight room was a routine that helped you
grow in terms of muscular capacity. As you stabilized that routine
in your life, you kept increasing in that capacity.

Whenever I start to feel depressed or when I feel that I'm
otherwise losing meaning in my life, I discover that I have slipped
out of some important routines. Self-evaluation, using my daily
life strategy checklist (reprinted at the start of this letter), helps get
me back on track.

At the top of my list of routines are exercising and diet. In the
warm months I walk several miles every day with your mother,
and I also often walk eighteen holes of golf while carrying my golf
bag. I tend to get into very good shape. During these months I
tend to also control what I eat. Then all of a sudden, I lose it, usually in November. When it gets cold, I stop going outside. I stop
exercising. I get depressed and start eating like a bear preparing for
hibernation. I quickly put on ten pounds, and I stop exercising.
I am suddenly "free" from the disciplines of the summer. When

this happens, I am not as sharp. I tend to dislike myself. I have more difficulty getting into the extraordinary being state. If I decide to analyze myself, problems with exercise and diet often become obvious issues. To turn things around, I often make new commitments around exercise and diet routines. It is not until I start to keep those commitments that I feel better. Reason, analysis, discipline, and structure now move me to responsible freedom, and I begin to grow and feel better about myself.

Over the past ten years, as my body has begun to age, I have watched many of my physical capabilities decline. For this reason, I have found golf to be an important activity. For me golf is a Zen-like activity. It is about the only sport that my body can tolerate. It is very demanding and requires great discipline to make any progress. Slowly and with much frustration, the progress comes. I find that physical progress to be very joyful. I am getting better at something. By increasing the commitment and discipline, I increase in the capacity to create. If I do not work on golf or some other aspect of physical development, I tend to get down on myself. So when I am down, I often make new commitments in this area. The commitments are tools that structure my energy toward a positive end.

Mental disciplines are extremely important to me. When I am involved in a systematic program of study, I feel my mind expand. It is increasing in capacity just as exercise increases the capacity of my physical body. I love learning. Many times I get caught up in the travel demands and other busy activities of my life and notice that I have not been learning. I often have to make new commitments to study and research. For people your age, I think it is hard to identify with this item. In school, study was something imposed. In college, you end up in a set of random courses imposed by the requirements of the college. You end up with teachers who vary in quality. Study tends to be drudgery. My advice is to look for ways to take charge of your own education. Ask what result you want to create. Identify a promising path, any path. Then bring discipline to your energy. Learning is a great experience, one that has brought great joy into my own life and I guess as your father I want to share that source of joy with you.

Prayer is something people do not talk about much, though this has been an important part of my life. There are many forms of prayer. Most often we think of it as a direct conversation with God. In the movies it is often seen as a superficial or crisis-based conversation with God—the so-called foxhole convert situation, where a person prays that his or her own life will be spared. I think it takes great discipline to make prayer a deep and searching two-way conversation. It means disciplined talking and disciplined listening. Not much emphasis is put on the listening part. For me the best form of prayer happens when I combine scripture study, reflection, and writing. It is then that I feel that God speaks to me and through me. Prayer is a great routine, and it is easy to get out of the routine or to slip into superficial patterns. Here again I often have to make a conscious effort to recommit myself.

Closing integrity gaps is a routine that goes with prayer. It takes disciplined reflection and prayer for me to get past my defenses and see my own hypocrisy. Now, we are all hypocrites, and we are all experts at hiding from our own hypocrisy. This is the very thing that most keeps us from growing. Once I am able to see my hypocrisy, my sense of shame drives me to change. Examining and closing integrity gaps is a routine that will empower people faster than anything else I know. When I am down, I try to get very honest with myself about my lack of honesty. It often makes a very big difference.

Finally, there's the challenge of family life, which demands discipline of still another kind. The professional world is designed to destroy family. Family life is very real and very painful. The family is a great clinic for teaching us how to live with intimacy and love. If we can succeed in the family, we can succeed elsewhere. Yet the pain of disciplining ourselves to live successfully with the family is real, and the call of the professional world is seductive. I like the quote "No success in life compensates for failure in the home." It boils things down to the essence. Many people use professional life as the excuse as they watch their families collapse. You have seen many tragic cases. I have sometimes allowed myself to get pulled out of fulfilling my role in the family, as you know. When this happens, quality goes out of my relationships with those I love most. Reviewing this item on my checklist is very helpful indeed. It forces me to increase my self-discipline and do the things I need to do.

Caring for our family and serving others are similar in their impact on our lives and the lives of those with whom we interact. I often get very self-focused. I get immersed in my tasks. The ultimate challenge for me has always been how to be productive while also being other-focused. When I am working hard but loving the people around me, my life is immensely rich and rewarding. When I feel that I am doing something to serve other people rather than myself, it also makes a very big difference. The fact that I am focusing this letter on you has greatly enriched the task. When I am down, I often find it helpful to check how much I am focused on serving the needs of other people. If I discover that I have become too self-focused I try to shift my attention to others immediately. This is hard, and I often fail.

Saving mornings for creative work is a wonderful discipline for me, and I highly recommend it. I have a friend who is a world-renowned scholar in the social sciences. He is incredibly productive. As I came to know him well, I learned that he gets up at four every morning and does his reading and writing. At noon he goes in and holds meetings and teaches. He calls the morning his "golden hours." Years ago I thought that was extreme. Now I employ that very same pattern. If I save the morning for my most creative tasks, the rest of my life falls in place. If I let the business of the world intrude on my mornings for more than a couple of days in a row, I lose my sense of creative productivity. I believe that most people could implement this idea to a much greater extent than they think is possible. When I have control of my mornings and when I get important creative tasks done, my days go much better.

Related to all of the foregoing is the issue of controlling our commitments. In the professional world, the more successful you get, the more demands there are on your time. Initially you think the opportunities are wonderful, but soon you become controlled by external agendas. You lose sense of who you are. You no longer have time to do the things that made you successful in the first place. The joy goes out of your world. It takes great discipline to say no to opportunities, particularly if the opportunities involve financial rewards. The only way I know how to control commitments is to be extraordinarily clear about who I am and highly disciplined around my priorities. I have to be able to say no to very enticing things and to very intense social pressures. I have to choose to be internally driven. Often when I get down, it is because I am sinking into a schedule of commitments and demands that serve random external purposes. At that point I have to recognize what's happening and take control of my time.

Focusing professionally is difficult. In my job there are three general activities: teaching, research, and consulting. Within each category are many different forms of activities, with a variety of demands around each form. It's easy to get spread very thin. It is critical to know my professional purpose, know what projects will advance that purpose, and then exercise the discipline to pursue the most productive and fulfilling path. Often I do not, and I start to feel like I am losing something. Here again I often feel better after refocusing myself.

In modern life, discipline around money has become more important than perhaps at any other time in history. Money is like time. There are many demands on it. Those demands can deplete the supply. People who do not have clear financial priorities and a disciplined budget often end up in turmoil, having to sacrifice their freedom to pay off their debts. The first key for me is to remember that money is a means and not an end. Money is not a measure of my personal value. If I am clear about my life purpose, I can be clear about how much money I need. If I can control my desires, I can often live on less money and therefore live a more peaceful life. In sum, when my finances are under control, my life is better.

Playing is an item many people forget. A few years ago I organized an unusual panel at the National Academy of Management Meetings. It was about living through the last phases of one's career. I invited two good friends who had cancer to take part. When they spoke, it came from the center of their soul, and everyone listened. The one thing that both of them said is that they are now much more disciplined about playing. One definite pattern they regret about their past careers is that they did not take enough time to play.

I came to the same conclusion when one of my colleagues had a heart attack. He and I had similar schedules. His coronary really made me stop and evaluate what I was doing in my own life. I decided to become much more systematic about play. For several years I have put considerable time into playing. The paradox is that since doing that, I have been more productive and more creative than at any other point in my career. The need to be busy, to be continuously working, is a fear-driven myth. We do not have to buy into it. When I am down, it is always useful for me to check up on my routines around play.

Notice that the checklist of positive routines is a checklist of positive disciplines. They make my life better because they bring structure to the expression of my energy. When my energy is moving through these structures, it gets converted into more positive outcomes and impacts. When I see the more positive outcomes and impacts, I get excited. I feel more energy. Responsible freedom means I multiply myself. I feel better about myself. Conversely, if I get trapped in patterns of self-defeating behaviors, if I embrace the negative addictions discussed earlier, my energy is dissipated. It goes for naught. Instead of seeing positive outcomes, I see myself causing tragic patterns that are so painful, I must deny the reality I see. I begin to live in a false world, and in such a world I have difficulty accessing energy. As I embrace foolish freedom, I watch myself choose slow death. When I embrace responsible freedom, I enter the extraordinary being state and rejoice in life.

Let me take this notion to a higher level of analysis. Consider one other statement from your last letter:

> I see coaches all the time who do not make the most of
> the players around them. I've watched many teams with
> great players who were mediocre because of their coach.
> On the other hand, there are the Princeton-type teams who
> have only mediocre players but a great system and a great
> coach who gets the most from his players.

This is a wonderful observation. It really made me think, because it is such a great example of leading change. Some coaches never tap the full potential of their talent, while other coaches get their teams to exceed their talent. The latter coaches know how to lead change. For a team to succeed, it must change. It must evolve from a collection of self-interested individuals to an integrated team with capacity, skill, and commitment. The players must learn to practice responsible freedom. This happens by bringing structure and discipline to energy. The great coach brings a great system to the players he or she has, and they become integrated with the system. Great coaches can lead change because they have learned how to differentiate and integrate positive values. Most have learned this because they, in their personal lives, have chosen to grow. They, like you, have moved through the stages of change. They have experienced victory over self. They understand the negative zone and the extraordinary being state. They understand the nature of potential and how to call it forth. In short, they have learned to apply a framework of Wholonics constructs that I am starting to share with you. In the meantime, I hope you find these ideas helpful. I love you with all my heart.

Dad

Use the Wholonics Constructs

Dear Garrett,

When I was writing the last letter to you, the words just seemed to flow. I felt integrated with you and full of love for you. As I wrote, I felt that the words might have a positive value in your life. That excited me. I am delighted that you found the letter to be the most enjoyable one yet. Your response increases my joy. I was particularly interested in your comments about the value of the spiral model of change and your analysis of your own motivation.

> *The first part I wanted to talk about was the model that the three researchers developed. I felt that I could relate to the steps. I have definitely gone through the precontemplation stage and the contemplation stage. I might have dipped into the preparation and action stages a little, but if I had, then I definitely have relapsed into the earlier stages. I guess I am moving forward and backward like the model says. I think that as I do that, I am learning more about myself so, maybe I am growing and preparing to succeed. I do not know. I think I am less discouraged than I was, but I am still discouraged. The idea of relapse seems important. When I was reading the letter, I was thinking that the model of self-change wasn't right—until I came to the part where you say that people often relapse. That made me a little more comfortable with the model. While I'm still not sure if I have even made it as far as you think I have, I know I have contemplated change. That is the good part. The bad part is that I haven't made any effort to take the steps necessary to change. I'm stuck, and I'm not sure why, but I feel comfort-*

able in the state that I'm in, even though I'm not truly
happy. It seems as if I don't want to change because I like the
attention. Sometimes it is nice to think of all the people that
are worried about me. This is very selfish, but it's the truth.

You indicate that you have not progressed as far as I think, that you have not even decided to change. While that may be true, there are many things in your letter that suggest you are in the process of changing. For one thing, you letter is full of powerful self-insights. I see fewer rationalizations and more engagement with reality. For example, you said that you felt comfortable in the state you are in, even though you were not truly happy. You said that it seemed like you didn't want to change because you liked the attention you were getting, that sometimes it was nice to think of all the people that were worried about you. You engage a very powerful reality when you recognize that you are not truly happy. That is a courageous statement. You also note an important motivational issue. You note that one of the payoffs of living in an unhappy pattern is that you draw much attention from those who love you. Family therapists talk about this in terms of "attention theory."

People desperately need attention or relationship. The self develops and grows in relationship. Just as babies who are deprived of physical touch tend to die, so people who are deprived of attention tend to die psychologically. For this reason people are often willing to go to extremes to get attention. Children will often deviate from family values and expectations so that they can get more attention. In my letter about the extraordinary being state I talked about deviance. The deviance on the left side of the normal curve is negative deviance, as opposed to the positive deviance on the right side of the curve. When people are hungry for attention, one way to get it is to deviate, to violate the normal values and expectations. The easiest way to get attention is to deviate in the negative direction.

I am reminded of that infamous day in our family history when Kristin was about twelve, when she fell down the stairs. No one realized it until she started to yell. She told us she could not move. We told her we were going to have to call the ambulance. She told us to go ahead. The medics took her to the hospital, where she spent hours going through tests. Ten years later she finally told us that when she landed at the bottom of the steps and no one came to help, she decided that it was about time that she got some attention. So she started screaming and faked the entire episode. I must admit she was wise to wait ten years to tell us.

Not all stories are as funny as that one. As people become hungry for attention, they often deviate in ways that are very costly to themselves. Think about some of the groups you encountered in high school and some of the things that people did to develop identities in those groups. Think about those two kids who shot up the high school in Colorado. Think how far they deviated and the tragic cost that everyone paid.

The need for attention and the need for rebellion often go hand in hand. In my last letter I discussed foolish freedom. The price of foolish freedom can be very high. In your letter you talked about how, when you were younger, you placed much value on having great willpower. You thought that willpower was everything and that you were strong because you resisted all the immoral temptations that came your way. But then you said, "I now realize that my will is weak. I am not as strong as I thought, and I am not as smart as I thought." You went on to say that you were haunted by this realization and that somehow you felt they "planted seeds of laziness and procrastination" in you.

I think we often make choices that result in self-defeating patterns. As you indicate, like the rest of us, you have practiced foolish freedom. In your case the positives—willpower and intelligence—were linked with the negatives—laziness and procrastination. Had the positives of willpower and intelligence been integrated with the positives of purpose and commitment, I suspect that the past year of your life would have been more satisfying. You would have continued to be a positive deviant and would still have enjoyed plenty of attention, although positive deviants usually need very little attention. Their rewards come from pursuing the purpose, from doing the task itself. The rewards are internal. It is as we disconnect from reality and enter slow death that our need for attention goes up.

Slow death is on my mind today. I am writing this in Istanbul. It is a beautiful day, and I am looking out on a panoramic view of the Black Sea. Two days ago I toured the city and was impressed with a history that went back not just centuries but millennia. Istanbul is one of the pivot points of the world, a strategic location where East meets West. On the tour I saw artifacts and heard stories about the evolution of religion, war, trade, and technology. I was impressed by the drama of the great human story, the coming together of differentiated peoples, the clash of cultures, and the acting out of human possibility.

What impressed me as I toured the area was how clear it became that the human story is not linear. It is more like the spiral model of self-change. Human progress moves forward and backward but it keeps moving up. In exploring the history of Istanbul, I kept thinking about that early letter in which I describe the two movies *First Contact* and *Contact*. In each one, cultures collide. The story of Istanbul is the story of cultures in collision. The story of business is the story of cultures in collision. The stories of your life and my life and all lives are the stories of colliding and evolving value systems. We move forward, fail, learn, and once again move forward. Perhaps the worst thing we can do is get discouraged and quit. Remember, *"life only passes you by when you give up on your abilities to change."* When we stop learning and changing, we get into a vicious cycle and begin to hate ourselves. We feel best when we are growing and contributing.

In normal experience, getting to contribution is a challenge. It takes leadership. Remember in my first letter I pointed out that almost everyone wants to make a difference. In this letter I would like to focus on leadership, or *how* to make a difference. I would like to propose a way to think about leadership that is new. I call it "Wholonics leadership." If you can grasp it and use it, I think it would be of considerable value to you. It will help you live more frequently in the state of contribution.

When it comes to contribution, most groups and organizations fail to meet their potential. For example, I am here in Istanbul to work with a pharmaceutical company. The directors want me to help them think about how to change in the direction of increased cooperation. They have tried to launch programs to increase the speed of their operation. Yet these efforts have not been successful because various groups in the organization find the proposed changes to be contrary to the company's immediate self-interests. As this organization evolved, many units were differentiated so that they operate like little fiefdoms, with their own interests, values, and cultures. Because each of these defends its self-interests, internal competition and conflict are rife. My experience suggests that this is not the exception but the rule.

Most groups and organizations do not live up to their potential because the individuals do not get lifted above their self-interests. I often say, if I had to reduce thirty years of learning about organizations to one sentence, it would be this: "It is natural for human beings to seek their self-interests." The result is that most organizations and most teams are like the pharmaceutical company. They are full of internal competition, and this competition ultimately weakens the whole or even destroys it.

It takes a leader to transform a group from patterns of self-interested conflict to cohesive, focused effort. We call such people transformational leaders because they turn groups or organizations into high-performing systems. A good example is the story of Pat Riley coaching the New York Knicks, a team that was riddled with internal competition and warring cliques. The competition between the cliques led the players to define each other negatively and provided justification for more competition between them. They became trapped in a vicious cycle.

One day Riley made an intervention that transformed the team. He stood up and named the members of each clique and the characteristics of each clique. He had them rearrange their chairs and sit in their cliques. The exercise was simple but very graphic. Riley was communicating his message at a level that everyone could understand. He was showing his players the emergent reality that they were choosing to create but did not want to see. This kind of feedback always stimulates anger—and they were angry. They did not enjoy looking at their own foolish freedom. He talked to them about positive values like tolerance, openness, and team spirit, values that lead to the integration of oppositions.

At the outset the Knicks were surviving, but they were heading toward slow death. They needed to be reinvented. Riley's intervention was one dramatic moment in a much larger pattern of transforming the team and ultimately leading them into the playoffs. Only a few coaches and a few executives are, like Riley, transformational. They help others transcend self-interest to refocus on the purpose of their own lives or their organizations' lives and make a contribution that nurtures human possibility.

Entropy pulls us toward differentiation and disintegration. We must work to overcome it. Humankind progresses as groups and organizations and great cultures come together and interpenetrate. Individuals grow when they feel that they are learning and contributing to a higher purpose. For this to happen, differentiations must be integrated. Integration of differentiated humans requires a transformational leader.

Hundreds of empirical studies on transformational leadership have been conducted, and they have yielded some definitive conclusions. First, most people are not transformational. They are authority figures who practice what social scientists call "contingent-reward leadership." This simply means that the manager's key assumption is that the people are self-interested. The manager must therefore control their behavior. The authority figure does this by clarifying objectives and then specifying rewards and punishments that will be assigned according to how well each employee meets or fails to meet expectations. Many senior people, like CEOs or generals, are called leaders because they hold the position at the top of their organization, but they are not true leaders; they are managers who preserve value. To create value one must be transformational.

The transformational leader recognizes that people are self-interested but refuses to accept that as inevitable. The transformational leader moves people from self-interest to collective interest. Such a leader understands that rewards, punishments, and controls simply keep people in the reactive stance and prevent them from increasing their sense of self-worth. The objective is to help people develop genuine involvement in the tasks they do. This is termed authentic commitment. In the end, these leaders get people to do more than they intended, sometimes more than they thought possible. How do leaders do this?

They increase trust by modeling authentic commitment. They can be counted on to do the right thing, to have integrity, to be morally sound. They are also deeply engaged in the pursuit of the purpose, leading the way in the work. To be authentic and engaged is to have authentic commitment. They literally model the authentic commitment they want from others. Pat Riley modeled such commitment when he raised the anger of his team.

Second, transformational leaders arouse people and cause them to become mindful, to consider new possibility. These leaders provide meaning, envision alternative futures, and show enthusiasm, optimism, and inspiration. Yet they also exercise reason and analysis; they think deeply and see unusual patterns. They thus preserve order while embracing change. They integrate reality and possibility, the past and the future. They provide a grounded vision that calls people to a purpose higher than self. Riley also did this.

Third, transformational leaders continually question assumptions by identifying patterns, reframing possibilities, and stimulating others to do the same. They model risk taking, remain open to new ideas, and encourage others to be open and to try new things. Yet they are not seen as wild and capricious. They are seen as consistent and stable, and they also provide a consistently supportive and safe context in which others can risk and innovate. That is, transformational leaders are both open and secure; they practice adaptive confidence, which is the ability to move forward into the face of uncertainty trusting that we will learn and move just as the spiral model of change suggests. Riley did not have the final answers, but recognized that his players had to move to a higher level of functioning.

Finally, transformational people have high standards and do not waver from them. In this sense they practice contingent reward leadership, yet they expand it by showing a great deal of individualized consideration by supporting people, listening, coaching, and mentoring. They both challenge and praise; they practice tough love. Riley was doing exactly this.

There are two kinds of transformational leaders: pseudotransformational leaders and real transformational leaders. The primary difference is in their motivational system. Pseudoleaders seek their own interests. "Self-concerned, self-aggrandizing, exploitative, and power-oriented, pseudotransformational leaders believe in distorted utilitarian and warped moral principles," writes Bernard Bass. Genuine transformational leaders transcend their own self-interests. They make sacrifices for the good of the group or because of some moral principle that calls them to a higher level of purpose. The phrase I use to summarize this is that transformational people are "internally directed and other-focused."

Given our discussion of survival, it is important to note one other thing: that transformational leaders transcend normal assumptions, even the most powerful of our normal assumptions, including survival and self-interest. Ronald Heifetz notes that leadership means to go forth to die. He also proposes an explanation: "Perhaps because warfare has played a central role historically in the development of our conceptions of leadership and authority, it is not surprising that the ancient linguistic root of the word *lead* means *to go forth to die*."

I would suggest an alternative explanation. To lead does mean to go forth to die, in two ways. First, transformational leadership requires ego death. When we remove the ego, our consciousness is transformed because it becomes enlarged by our unconscious. We become one. We are reborn. We become new. When this happens, the meaning of life changes. We see our purpose not as consumption but as contribution. We become deeply committed to moving ourselves and others up the spiral of life. As this commitment deepens, we reach a level where physical survival is less important than the purpose for which we live. The fear of death is no longer our prison. We are willing to suffer or even die for our cause. Survival is no longer the first law of nature. For such a person, the first law of nature is contribution. If the greatest contribution we can make is our own failure, humiliation, expulsion, firing, or death, then we make it. This fact is far outside the reactive, fear-driven reality of normal life. It is extremely difficult for people. They resist it. To accept it is to accept the accountability to live life to the fullest. Most people do not see the profound possibilities in their lives, and most are not fully alive.

When Pat Riley did what he did, he knew that the team members would be furious. He was willing to suffer that anger anyway. Why? He saw possibilities and potential in his players that they could not see in themselves. He was willing to take the risks and suffer the consequences necessary for them to transform. He was willing to go forth to die.

At the business meeting here in Istanbul, the leader of the company stood up and announced a dramatic change in policy that would affect the lives of every person present. He explained that it was necessary for the organization to survive financially. The announcement had a great impact. It required that everyone consider making great sacrifices. There was much grumbling throughout the first day. It was hardly a positive context for discussing cooperation. The organizers were worried that the entire meeting would be a waste.

When it was my turn to speak, I asked them all to complete the following phrase: "The reason I love this company is . . ." After they wrote their answers, I went around and had about twenty people read what they wrote. I then asked the leader of the company to summarize the answers. He did so. Three themes were expressed: they loved the people, the opportunities, and the task itself. I went on and gave them a framework and a set of tools for achieving greater cooperation. At the end I spoke of the greatness of what the people in the room had accomplished. I reviewed many of the great medical breakthroughs they had made and how their contributions would never be erased. I then asked them to think about why it is that we compete in the world of business, why hard financial risks are taken, and why everyone in the room was asked to suffer. The answer is that we compete not to survive but we compete to survive so that we can contribute. The organization is a form through which we can know our own greatness. It is a form through which we can push others up the great spiral of life. That insight seemed to change everything. The grumbling attitude was gone. The room was filled with excitement and possibility. These business leaders were beginning to integrate the notions of survival and profound possibility.

As I read your last letter, I saw profound possibility. You have become aware of the price you have been paying for foolish freedom. You are no longer denying it. You are more like the New York Knicks after Pat Riley did his exercise. Many of us deny that we practice foolish freedom and never grow past it. I often find myself in this state. I simply stay in the precontemplation stage. In contrast, you are moving forward. I think there are some tools that might help you to continue to move forward.

In my life statement is a section I call my Self-Empowering Questions. It contains five questions, my "five keys to profound possibility." I often use them, particularly when the chips are down, to call forth my best self:

What result do I want to create?
Am I practicing authentic commitment?
Am I practicing grounded vision?
Am I practicing adaptive confidence?
Am I practicing tough love?

Let me illustrate how these questions can transform who I am. A few months ago I had a very, very bad day. I was in charge of our first executive education conference at the Michigan Business School. The program included many of our most visible faculty members. The program was being marketed to business leaders all over the world. It was to be a very exciting weeklong event. We began planning a year in advance. For ten months everything went very smoothly. Two months before the event, we had sold half the available seats. This fit perfectly with the assumptions of our marketing people. They told us that 50 percent of the attendees would sign up during the last three weeks.

One day one of our marketing people told us that perhaps the assumption about the percentage of people who would sign up during the last three weeks was wrong. He had talked to an experienced outside colleague who said the assumption did not fit our kind of conference. The number of attendees we had six weeks before was pretty much what we would have. This news was stunning. If this was true, the conference would be a disaster. It would be an embarrassment to the school, the faculty, and the attendees.

As I drove home, my stomach was in knots. I began to explore the consequences of every dark possibility. My sense of panic increased. I was filled with self-doubt. I remembered something I had forgotten for a while: I was a loser. I had always known this, but now the secret was going to be exposed to the rest of the world.

When I went to bed, I could not sleep. I got up and went to my study. I paced the floor. As I did so, I remembered a conversation that took place in that very room. It was the conversation that I described in an early letter, the one in which I asked Shauri if she was problem-solving or purpose-finding. I pondered that question for a moment and then pulled out my life statement and reread it. I eventually came to the part that lists the five questions.

As had happened a number of times in the past, these questions had an immediate effect on me. I asked myself what result I wanted to create. Quickly I recognized that filling seats was a problem, not a purpose. The purpose was to learn how to build a quality product that would be in demand year after year. We were doing this not to fill seats and look good. We were doing this as a project in action learning. We wanted to learn how to put on a great conference on a consistent basis. We do such learning by moving forward under uncertainty and running action experiments. We were trying to move up the great spiral. This insight brought some relief.

The next four questions raised issues about my relationship to that desired result (I will explain them in just a moment). As I answered them, I went from relief to excitement. I began to write notes. In a few moments the knots left my stomach. An hour later I went to bed and slept nicely. In the morning I went to my computer and started to type a message to our conference staff. Ideas began to flow, new ideas that I had not had the night before. By the time I was finished, a positive plan of action was in place.

At that point I noticed two things. First, I again felt some confidence. That brought a feeling of peace. Second, I was amazed at the difference in me. Less then twelve hours earlier, I was living in a state of hopeless fear. Now I was a different person. I had asked myself some simple questions and they led to a change in my being. I went from living in fear to living in possibility. My note to the staff was not full of problems to be solved; it was filled with positive propositions that might potentially ignite their energy. As I sat in my study writing, I was producing the resources necessary to help the staff to move through uncertainty with confidence. As they did so, they would learn their way into the new and desired future. Since I was being change, I was leading change.

When leading change, we are moving forward in the face of uncertainty. In such a process, we can never know beforehand where we will end up. In the case at hand, the conference came off almost perfectly. Everyone who participated felt it was a quality event. We made no profit on the conference, but we learned how to move forward in designing such a product in future years. It is vital that as we move forward in the face of uncertainty, we continually learn, continually clarify, and continually exhibit our courage. When we do, we attract others forward in the learning process.

I would like to describe what is behind the last four questions, why they had such an impact on me, and how you could use them in a similar way. But first, we need to be clear about an important issue. In an earlier letter I asked "What is an effective organization?" and answered by rewriting a paragraph about entropy. Here I would like to ask, "What is an effective me?" and I would like to answer by again rewriting the same paragraph.

I desire to live in my comfort zone. I am thus normal. To be normal is positive, but clinging to my comfort zone often leads me to become a victim of entropy. Entropy is "evil" in the sense that I begin to conspire in my own slow death. To avoid entropy, I must focus my attention on "work to be done." "Good" is action that "preserves the order" in me while "preventing rigidity." "Good" is action that integrates stability and change and thus continually integrates the past and the future so as to give focus to the present. It is action that produces value while maintaining meaning, action that thus continually integrates my purpose and processes. Such integrated action must be "informed by the needs of the most evolved systems," and it must "take into account the future, the common good." It must include an awareness of the "well-being" of other systems in which and with which I exist.

So an effective me is a person who is working to learn and grow in more effective service to others. It is a me that does not quit because I am immobilized by the threatening events that occur around me. It is a me that has core values. Since those values can compete with one another, I must continually work to integrate them so that I am not led into rigidity or other negative states. If I do allow myself to stagnate, I will become depressed and lose energy. I must refuse to be *dammed* or *damned*. I must keep moving. I must know my purpose and strive to be both stable and growing. My past and future must become connected in a coherent story.

Unfortunately, I am not always my best self. I love being in my comfort zone, and I work to stay there. The result is that I often get caught in the process of slow death or entropy. My spirit sags, and I get discouraged and depressed. Yet I would rather live with these negative emotions than face the terror of moving forward under uncertainty.

The four questions help me live in possibility. They are focused on four constructs: authentic commitment, grounded vision, adaptive confidence, and confrontation, or tough love. These constructs were invented through the use of Wholonics reasoning.

Let me say a little more about Wholonics reasoning. In an earlier letter I talked about Chuang Tzu and the ancient insights into paradox. Part of the argument in that tradition is that once you identify and label a category, you lose truth. Truth is not in the label but in the processes of reality. In the processes of reality, particularly processes of interpenetration when the soil and the acorn become one, our labels are often violated. Remember the example of person-oriented and task-oriented leadership. The labels blinded researchers to the fact that transformational leaders are high on both. The ancient tradition suggests that truth can be discovered only intuitively. We have to "build the bridge as we walk on it." Well, I invented Wholonics reasoning to help identify or invent new concepts, concepts or constructs that marry conceptual, positive opposites so as to allow us to see clearly what we normally cannot see at all, the process of interpenetration and transformation.

Here I will give you four such constructs. They reflect the four questions asked earlier. They were invented by taking a list of eight virtues or positive values and applying Wholonics reasoning. The eight are integrity, reason, confidence, selflessness, engagement, hope, humility, and assertiveness. There is nothing sacred about this particular list. Other positives could have been employed. As you read about them, you will note that they are consistent with my review of the empirical research on transformational leadership. Although the data show the opposing positive characteristics to be present in transformational leadership, no one has ever presented them in such a fashion. I doubt that many people notice the positive oppositions. Researchers tend to think about transformation in relatively linear ways.

Authentic commitment is the first construct. Here there are two differentiated positive values in relationship: the first is integrity; the second is engagement. To have integrity is to live a principled life, to be virtuous, to be an authentic or real person. In many spiritual traditions it is suggested that we find our integrity by withdrawing from the world. We should retreat to the nunnery, the Buddhist monastery, to a forty-day fast in the wilderness. The assumption is that we become pure by withdrawing from the corruption of the world. The problem with this perspective is that we may so cherish our integrity that we lose our connectedness.

In attempting to maintain our purity, we may become aloof, withdrawn, or detached.

The opposite of avoidance is engagement. A person who is engaged is involved, connected, and committed. A person who it too involved, however, may lose perspective and integrity. That person may become corrupted, polluted, and compromised. This negative state is the opposite of integrity. The challenge is for me to integrate these highly differentiated positive values, to hold them in profound contact. The challenge is to be principled and involved, virtuous and engaged, authentic and committed. The challenge as stated by many spiritual traditions is to "be in the world but not of the world." I call this authentic commitment.

Authentic commitment represents an interpenetration of two positive but highly differentiated values (see the accompanying table). When I pursue an integration of these two values, I tend to enter a being state in which I am deeply involved; my involvement is based on a pure motive. That is, I am doing what I am doing because it is inherently right, not because of the external rewards or punishments it might bring. I am doing the task for the sake of the task. I am intensely involved, inner-directed, and other-focused. Authentic commitment is a very powerful construct. When you choose authentic commitment, you immediately change, and so does the world.

Here is an illustration. You may remember that when you read *Change the World*, I told the story of a man who attended my Leading Change course at the Michigan Business School. It is a story that deserves repeating here because it perfectly illustrates authentic commitment. The man was a company president. During the first three days of the course, he said very little. On Thursday morning, he asked if we might have lunch together, and I agreed. Over lunch he told me that if he had attended my course at any time in the previous five years, he would have been wasting

Authentic Commitment.

Vice: Avoidance	Virtue: Integrity	Interpenetration: Authentic Commitment	Virtue: Engagement	Vice: Corruption
Aloof	Principled	Principled and involved	Involved	Corrupted
Withdrawn	Virtuous	Virtuous and engaged	Connected	Polluted
Detached	Authentic	Authentic and committed	Committed	Compromised

his time. He had successfully turned around two companies and felt he knew everything there was to know about leading change.

Then he pointed out that he was now a lot more humble. There were five companies in his corporation. He had turned two of them around and was seen as the shining star among the presidents. He had earned the right to lead the largest company in the corporation. The current president of that largest company still had, however, eighteen months left until his retirement. In the meantime, he had been asked to try his hand at one more turnaround. There was a company in the corporation that was considered hopeless. It had once commanded a large market share for its product. Today, it had only a small slice of the market and was still shrinking. Nobody believed this company could be turned around, so if he failed in his efforts, no one would hold it against him.

It had now been twelve months since he took on the challenge. He felt defeated. Everything that had worked for him before, everything his past had taught him, failed in the present situation. Morale was dismal. The numbers were dismal. The outlook for the future was dismal.

I asked him what he thought he would do next. On a paper napkin he listed his short-term objectives. He began to draw an organizational chart. He described the people in each of the senior positions and described the assignments and changes he was going to make in regard to each person on the chart. I found his answer unexciting. There was no commitment or passion in what he was telling me. Yet it was clear that he was a man of character with a sincere desire to succeed. I took a deep breath and asked a hard question.

"What would happen if you went back and told those people the truth? Suppose you told them that you have been assigned as a caretaker for a year and a half. No one believes the company can succeed, and no one really expects you to succeed. You have been promised the presidency of the largest company, and the plan is to put you into that plum job. Tell them that you have, however, made a fundamental choice. You have decided to give up that plum job. Instead, you are going to stay with them. You are going to bet your career on them, and you invite them to commit all the energy and goodwill they can muster into making the company succeed."

I was worried that I might have offended him and half expected an angry response. He looked at me for a moment; then it was his turn to take a deep breath. To my surprise and relief, he said, "That is pretty much what I have been thinking." He paused, and in that moment I watched him make the fundamental decision. Almost immediately, he picked up the napkin and started doing a reanalysis. He said, "If I am going to stay, then this person will have to go, this person will have to be moved over here, and this person . . ."

As he talked, there was now an air of excitement in his words. Once he had made the fundamental decision to stay, everything changed. His earlier plans to move on to the larger company were suddenly scrapped. He had made a fundamental choice, and now he had a new life stance, a new outlook, and a new way to behave. The organization chart that made sense a few moments before now made no sense at all. None of the original problems had changed, but he had changed, and that made all the difference in the world.

When we act with authentic commitment, we stop just going through the motions and instead become engaged with a pure motive. We are deeply engaged, not for promised rewards or to avoid punishment, but because it is the right thing to be doing at the moment. We are internally driven. When we make authentic commitment, we change, our view of the world changes, and the world begins to change.

In your last letter, something you said illustrated authentic commitment. You said, "I don't like to open up to people who care about me." And you note how much easier it is to open up to strangers. I think many people would agree with you. Opening up to the people who are closest requires that we increase our vulnerability, and that is one of the most difficult forms of personal work. I was impressed with what you said, that in writing the letter you were going to "try and be completely honest about everything." In doing that, you became engaged with authenticity. It was a commitment to a very high level of work. I suspect that writing the letter was more beneficial than writing many of the other letters.

When I am my worst self, I do not feel very engaged in what I am doing, nor do I have much sense of integrity. In fact, I tend to lack both, and I become more externally driven and more self-focused. When I am my best self, the opposite tends to be true. My integrity radiates in such a way that others see it. I feel confident in myself. I feel worthy of good outcomes. I am less fearful of being judged by others and so am more willing to be vulnerable. I am

acting, not reacting. I am the one with a message. I embody
the message I am advocating; in fact, I am a living symbol of the
message. People recognize that and tend to pay attention. They
become mindful. They are encountering something unusual and
need to make sense of it. This integrity begins to draw people.
It connects me to them, and we begin to make profound contact.
Such relationships tend to increase my own commitment, and I
tend to become more highly engaged. When I am enacting my best
self, I am fully present. I have enthusiasm. I contribute new ideas.
I am persistent and tend not to pick up negative energy. When this
kind of engagement is linked to authenticity, I have two highly
differentiated values in profound contact. This integration gives
me energy and makes me attractive to others. I become a source of
information, but I also become a source of inspiration. Within this
aura of influence, people are tempted toward self-examination,
courage, and the making of fundamental choices.

The second construct is grounded vision. It is also an interpenetration of two virtues. One of the virtues is hope. Hope is a
state of positive intention. It is often associated with things like
optimism, faith, vision, and enthusiasm. A person who is hopeful,
visionary, and enthusiastic has a very positive life orientation.
Such a person sees future possibilities unfolding and helps bring
them about. People like this generally tend to see and want to
work toward the creation of a better world. They often radiate
a positive influence that can attract and uplift us.

Hope has much to do with leadership and change. One of the
primary characteristics of leaders is that they have vision. Leaders
have faith and hope in the vision and express enthusiasm about
it. Persons who lack this tend to become authority figures more
than leaders. The same is true of outstanding teachers: they have
a vision rather than just a plan. They teach not to *inform* but to
transform.

Hope can become negative, however. Individuals with a positive orientation can become impractical, even deluded and unrealistic, making choices strictly on the basis of hope rather than looking carefully at what's actually in front of them. They are not grounded in reality. Occasionally we meet people who exercise faith and hope in a superstitious base. The worst example of that would be gamblers who are always hopeful that they will strike it rich with the next turn of a card. The basis of their hope is fundamentally irrational, illogical, unreasonable, and unsound. Another example would be visionaries who are convinced that the world is going to radically change for the better in a specific year or on a specific day. Their hope, vision, and enthusiasm are built on a false foundation about an arbitrary date on the calendar.

The opposing virtue is reason. The reasonable person is logical, realistic, and practical. Such persons tend to look for facts. They seek out what is known and certain. We see such people as grounded and strong. They tend to focus less on future possibilities and more on past and present realities. When they hear an account or explanation, they ask, "Is this logical? Does this make sense?" They question things and want to see evidence. They are often very orderly and tend to think in a systematic fashion.

Taken too far, the emphasis on reason can become negative. A tone of hopelessness creeps in—that the future will be exactly like the past, for example. Individuals may become so focused on facts that they will not entertain conceptual possibilities; so focused on order that they become stagnant, so wedded to logic that they become pessimistic, cynical, and skeptical. The world they inhabit can therefore seem dark and hopeless.

This tension tends to emerge particularly in arguments between scientists and religionists. People of science listen to the statements of faith and hope and accuse the religionist of delusion and superstition. They ask, "Where is the physical evidence?" The religionist, in turn, listens to the factual criticisms and asks, "Where are faith, hope, and optimism?" In their arguments, one fails to value reason and fact, while the other fails to value optimism and vision. Yet in fact the scientist is always using hope and faith and the religionist is always using reason and logic. Neither could function without using both.

The challenge is to achieve grounded vision, to combine hope, faith, and optimism with and reason, logic, and practicality. Studies of creativity suggest that great insights do not come effortlessly. People work hard on an issue. They then withdraw and out of the unconscious mind comes the insight. That is, intuition, insight, and revelation tend to occur to people who are exercising both faith and firmness of mind.

A person with grounded vision tends to be optimistic and logical, visionary and realistic, enthusiastic and practical (see the accompanying table). Grounded vision is the capacity to access the deepest truths of present internal and external reality and integrate them with a meaningful image of a better future state so that the image continually pulls the individual and others into new patterns of action.

To have grounded vision means that we see below the surface and have a deep understanding of present reality. We have appreciation and reverence for the potential that lies at the core of the existing system. We also have a deep understanding of the external reality or larger systems that surround us. We can see a possible fit between the internal and external systems. We can see a better future, and we can explain it in a reasoned way that reaches people at an intuitive level. Others, in turn, resonate with the grounded vision because it is logically and emotionally true. Grounded vision means that we can do this same thing when no one else is involved. We create images that lift us out of our own comfort zone.

Grounded Vision.

Vice: Superstition	Virtue: Hope	Interpenetration: Grounded Vision	Virtue: Reason	Vice: Hopelessness
Impractical	Optimistic	Optimistic and logical	Logical	Pessimistic
Deluded	Visionary	Visionary and realistic	Realistic	Cynical
Unrealistic	Enthusiastic	Enthusiastic and practical	Practical	Skeptical

When I am enacting my best self, I tend to study the basic processes very carefully. I think we all do this at times, even if we do not like details. When we receive a love letter, for example, we usually do not read it and put it down. We read it very carefully. We look at the nuances of every sentence. We search for meaning in every word. We are focused and very conscious. We look deeply into the love letter. That is what Johnny Miller was doing when he studied the moment of contact between the club and the ball in the golf swing. Grounded vision includes using reason to deeply analyze the core processes at the heart of the present reality and then articulating a future consistent with that reality.

Here's an illustration: I was once invited to a church meeting at which a family was making a presentation. I was particular interested when I listened to the eighteen-year-old daughter. In the middle of her talk she held up a large, framed document. She said, "This is our family vision. Whenever we have contention or if we have to make a decision, we go back and read it, and then we know what to do." She read the vision. I was impressed and later asked her father about it. Her father, Rick DeVries, was a bank president at the time. He told me the family vision actually had its roots at work.

When he first arrived in Ypsilanti, Michigan, he could see enormous potential for moving his branch banks forward. He began to work with his people to see that same potential. He knew that he had to change the culture of the branches. He talked with his people about the potential he saw, but nothing seemed to change. The manager who was directly over the first-line people, the personal bankers, seemed to have particular difficulty catching the vision of what might be possible. Rick tried to help her set meaningful goals, but the process did not lead to change. There was no tangible connection, no profound contact between the present and the future.

One day in a meeting it dawned on him to step out of the box. He asked all the people present to close their eyes. He then, in very concrete terms, described the branch that he saw. He paused and asked them now to imagine that they were walking into the best branch bank in the world. He asked, "What do you see?" Each person was asked to then share this mental picture. He recorded what each person said and then wrote a two-page document integrating their various views on what an ideal branch is like.

When Rick shared the written version of this description with the staff, the result was dramatic. The vision was something the people could understand, own, and act on. It was something that could guide their behavior as they tried to make profound contact between the present and the future, the actual and the potential. It particularly influenced the key manager, who was struggling to understand what Rick had been trying to tell her. She now understood perfectly and became excited and committed. Things began to move forward.

This process not only invigorated Rick's people but also Rick himself. He was struck by how much difference it made. He frequently found himself thinking about what had happened and talked about it a great deal. He told his peers about it, yet they showed only limited interest. This baffled him. Yet that is consistent with my experience. People are not eager to deal with grounded vision. Most people resist deep clarification of purpose; they prefer to spend their time problem-solving. It requires less integrity and accountability.

Rick and his wife have five children. Raising a family of that size is a challenge. On one particularly contentious day it struck him that what worked at the bank might work at home. He told his family that he would like to hold a family meeting. When the time came, he put on some music, put some snacks on the table, and called all family members together. He told them that he had played a game at the bank and would now like to play it with the family. He asked everyone in the room to close their eyes and imagine the ideal home. Here is the vision that eventually emerged from that family meeting:

> We see a home that is beautiful, clean, and orderly. It is filled with wonderful aromas and inspiring music. It is a place where first things first *guides our daily actions. We see a home where the Spirit is strong, where love constantly abounds in word and in deed. It is a place where voices are always soft and kind and where gentleness, patience, and caring service are ever-present. We see a home where individually and collectively, all are focused on drawing closer to the Spirit and becoming more like the Savior. We see a home that is a creative learning environment where minds expand and spirits soar. It is a place that fosters health and fitness, a place where hard work is undertaken, and a place where difficult things are accomplished. It is a home where the finances are in order, schedules are coordinated, and valiant spirits strive to make a difference for good in all that they do. We see a home full of smiles, happiness, and fun, where life is packed*

with hallowed traditions and treasured memories. Always,
we see Heaven here on Earth and a family forever.

The day I heard his daughter's presentation was several years after the family vision was created. Rick told me how important this vision had become to the all members of the family. They reviewed it regularly. There had been many critical moments when conflicts were resolved and key decisions were made by returning to the vision. For the parents and each of the children, the vision was a living document, taking them from the present into the future in a way they could understand. Rick said, "Over time even our little ones have come to understand the vision, and they often refer to it."

When you were in high school, Garrett, I think you experienced grounded vision in basketball. Brian Townsend was very good at teaching you and the others to marry present reality with future possibility. In your senior year, after having won the state championship, you and the others were very different. When you talked about the state tournament, you could see the connection between the things you were doing and the outcome you wanted to create. Winning a second championship was a vivid image; it lived in your consciousness and energized your efforts. That image called forth your best basketball self.

When people choose to enact their best self, they begin to have a vibrant and clear vision of their lives. They deeply know the details while also feeling the potential and seeing the possibilities. Such people learn to simplify their lives. They not only share a vision but also feel motivated to pursue it. They focus on value-added activities that allow growth and progress. We are then affected in a very deep and grounded way. We experience victory over self and therefore feel that our actions are consistent with our core values. Our own faith and hope increase, and our sense of understanding and reason expand.

In summary, we need to combine hope and reason. We need to strive to be hopeful and logical, visionary and realistic, enthusiastic and practical. Grounded vision means we have a deep understanding of present reality. We see into the existing system and have a reverence for the potential that lies within it. The people participating in the system resonate with the vision because it is both factually and emotionally true for them.

This construct is also consistent with the empirical research on transformational leadership. Transformational leaders provide meaning; they envision alternative futures and demonstrate enthusiasm, optimism, and inspiration as they arouse people. They also exercise reason and analysis. They think deeply and see unusual patterns. They thus preserve order while embracing change. They integrate reality and possibility, the past and the future.

The concept of adaptive confidence is a marriage between confidence and humility. People who are confident believe in themselves. They do not doubt that they have the capacity to perform a given task. Confident people are secure, centered, and assured. It is possible, however, to be too confident. A person can become proud and suffer from hubris, conceit, or arrogance. Proud or arrogant individuals overrate their abilities and tend to lose the capacity to learn. They become rigid and closed, unable to make use of input and feedback. This often disconnects them from emerging reality. They use defense mechanisms such as denial to avoid adaptation and growth.

The positive opposite of such hubris or vain pride is humility. The dictionary suggests that humility is an awareness of one's shortcomings. A humble person is modest and temperate. Such a person tends to be open, receptive, and teachable. The virtue of humility, however, can be taken too far. The overly humble person becomes self-effacing, self-denigrating, filled with insecurity and fear. They may become apprehensive, weak, filled with anxiety, easily manipulated, unclear about their needs or opinions, even undependable and unreliable. Such persons can be skillful in other ways but are seldom self-reliant, confident, or able to take initiative.

When there is a balance between humility and confidence, we find a person who is modest and centered, open and self-assured, receptive and firm (see the accompanying table). It is a challenge to bring these seemingly contradictory qualities together, but the effort is well worth any sacrifices we might make along the way.

Think of adaptive confidence as the ability to face the unknown and continually move forward to cocreate a new reality. People who have adaptive confidence feel a hunger for personal and collective learning and development. They recognize that the most powerful learning is found in an improvisational process. They are secure enough to seek feedback on their successes as well as their failures. Persons with adaptive confidence can move forward in most situations, taking initiative, remaining open to feedback on these initiatives, and learning while moving. They are

Adaptive Confidence.

Vice: Insecurity	Virtue: Humility	Interpenetration: Adaptive Confidence	Virtue: Confidence	Vice: Pride (Hubris)
Weak	Modest	Modest and centered	Centered	Arrogant
Uncertain	Open	Open and assured	Assured	Closed
Insecure	Receptive	Receptive and secure	Secure	Rigid

simultaneously stable and changing. They live with their environment in a positive, creative tension. Often the adaptive-confident person and the environment appear to be cocreating each other.

You are enacting your best self whenever you practice adaptive confidence. You have humility and confidence. Here the definition of humility includes not just the normal notion of awareness of shortcomings but also the larger concept I discussed earlier of seeing things as they really are. Humility is acknowledging your shortcomings and strengths and recognizing that without connectedness to outside systems, you are nothing. It is being open and receptive to all the positives and negatives that make up reality, including both the positives and negatives that others hold concerning you.

My friend Bill Torbert has written about confidence. He argues that most forms of professional knowledge result in conditional confidence—confidence that you will act well as long as the situation doesn't violate your assumptions about it. People are trained. They learn what to do in a given situation. They learn how to be in control. If the situation changes, they are not in control. This usually leads to panic. Most people live to be in control, to be in their comfort zone. Yet if we want to grow, we must learn to move outside our comfort zone.

Bill claims that the alternative to conditional confidence is unconditional confidence. I consider that synonymous with adaptive confidence. According to Bill, it means that we are capable of discarding inaccurate assumptions and ineffective strategies even in the midst of an ongoing action. We are confident enough to act and humble enough to learn at the same time. Bill also has a recommendation on how to develop such confidence. He says that unconditional confidence increases as our integrity increases, and *we increase integrity by constantly monitoring our lack of integrity.* I find this a very striking observation.

Adaptive confidence is often linked with the observation of people performing at a very high level. Consider this description:

> Sometime look at a novice workman or a bad workman and compare his expression with that of a craftsman whose work you know is excellent and you'll see the difference. The craftsman isn't ever following a single line of instruction. He's making decisions as he goes along. For that reason he'll be absorbed and attentive to what he is doing even though he doesn't deliberately contrive this. His motions and the machine are in a kind of harmony. He isn't following any set of written instructions because the nature of the material at hand determines his thoughts and motions, which simultaneously change the nature of the material at hand. The material and his thoughts are changing together in a progression of changes until his mind is at rest at the same time the material is right.

Masters of any given activity deeply understand that activity. They have maps of the territory programmed into their heads. They see and know things intuitively that the less masterful do not. They frame and reframe strategies as they read changing cues. They are confident that at any given moment they will do the right thing. They thus move forward in confidence and humility. As they exercise adaptive confidence, people tend to make profound contact and then begin to cocreate the future. As Pirsig states, the "nature of the material at hand determines his thoughts and motions, which simultaneously change the nature of the material at hand. The material and his thoughts are changing together in a progression of changes until his mind is at rest at the same time the material is right." There is profound contact and profound possibility. In the process of making the profound contribution, both the creator and the created are altered.

Greatness flows through the actor and increases that person's humility and confidence.

Research on transformational leaders shows that they are intellectually stimulated; they continually question assumptions, identify patterns, and reframe possibilities. They also stimulate others by becoming models of risk taking and being open to new ideas, encouraging others to open up and try new things. Yet they are not seen as capricious. They are consistent and stable because of seven qualities: (1) they are driven by principles, (2) their vision is grounded, (3) their creative behaviors are challenging but comprehensible, (4) they provide a supportive and safe context in which others can risk and innovate, (5) they are simultaneously open and secure, (6) they practice adaptive confidence, and (7) they continually call forth adaptation and growth.

The next construct is tough love. It emerges from an interpenetration of two sets of virtues. The first is selfless love, patience, caring, or support. The actor shows consideration for other people and acts as a loving coach or mentor. Such love can be distorted into permissiveness, indulgence, and leniency. In such cases, we seek to protect others. We let others perform below their level of capability. We do this in the name of love. Yet our action is really motivated by ignorance and fear. We do not know how to hold others to a high standard, or we simply are afraid to do so.

The second set of virtues is highly differentiated, with the positive virtue being assertiveness. Here the leader is powerful, bold, and challenging, seeing what needs to be done and boldly challenging others to do it. Taken too far, assertiveness becomes oppression—overbearing, manipulative, and self-serving. I see this particularly illustrated by athletic coaches. So many believe that assertiveness is necessary to transform a team. Yet they cannot see that support is necessary at the same time. They become oppressive. The result is always negative.

The desired balance of virtues is to be tough and loving.
A person who practices tough love is patient and powerful, caring
and bold, selfless and challenging (see the accompanying table).
So we see that tough love is the leader's ability to put the welfare
of others selflessly ahead of personal interests while boldly and
unwaveringly challenging others to live up to a standard that he or
she is already modeling for them.

Here is an illustration. I am reminded of a conversation I
had with a student who played football for Bo Schembechler, the
charismatic coach at the University of Michigan. The young man
was a very big lineman. I asked him what he thought of Bo. He
replied, "Bo is the only person in the world that I will let kick me
in the butt—because I know he loves me." We expect authoritative
discipline from leaders on the football field, but we seldom think
of it as evidence of caring. We do not expect a big, tough lineman
to use the "L word." Yet he did. He even implies that it is love that
makes the confrontation acceptable.

When others are practicing tough love, they are in fact
supporting me, and I can feel their genuine love and concern.
But they do not baby me. They want to call forth my greatness.
For this to happen, I must become a more independent actor and

Tough Love.

Vice: Permissiveness	Virtue: Selflessness	Interpenetration: Tough Love	Virtue: Assertiveness	Vice: Oppression
Permissive	Patient	Patient and powerful	Powerful	Oppressive
Indulgent	Caring	Caring and bold	Bold	Overbearing
Lenient	Selfless	Selfless and challenging	Challenging	Self-serving

take increased accountability for some aspect of my life. For me to transform, I must be attracted outside my comfort zone. The others must disturb the patterns in my mind and behavior. They disturb the way I choose to see myself by asking me tough questions or by making tough statements. Such distortions cause me to think deeply. Such thinking causes me to see my own stagnation. I continually run from pain, so I choose slow death. I go to sleep in some part of my life. The change agent challenges me to awaken, to stretch to my full limits. A good coach, like Pat Riley or Brian Townsend, tends to do this continually. He or she is trying to get the individuals and the collective to stretch and grow, to learn adaptive confidence. A parent, scout leader, CEO, or president of a nation must do the same.

The four Wholonics constructs are keys to profound possibility. They help us act rather than be acted on. Our challenge is to live the good life, which means continually reinventing ourselves so as to create more and more value for the common good and the systems that surround us—in short, to be a contributor. Since we live in a world of oppositions, the challenge is first to work on the only oppositions over which we have total control: the oppositions within us. We need to enact integrated positive-positive values instead of negative-positive or negative-negative values.

Virtues become more powerful when they are combined in positive oppositions because they become dynamic concepts that move us up the spiral. When two positive oppositions come in contact, we have profound contact. In this case it is profound contact at the conceptual level. The Wholonics virtues are Janusian concepts. They force us to look in two positive directions at the same time. They capture our interest and then call us to action in the creative mode. When we strive to live them, we stop being reactive. We tend to bridle our wayward passions, channeling and directing that passion to actualize our vision. Instead of reacting, we focus on a result. This leads to victory over self. When we experience such victory, we are filled with positive emotions. We are better able to love ourselves and better able to love others. We feel more courageous and confident.

In this process, we do not eliminate our passions; we bridle them. "Bridle" in this context means to direct, control, or govern. We direct our passions so that they have productive impact on the world and on us. We become filled with positive emotions. We enact our best self and model all the Wholonics virtues. We can then draw out the best self in others. We then join in a community of profound contact and clarify what it means to make a profound contribution.

The accompanying figure is a simple representation of the questions I have discussed. For me these questions are themselves transformational. If I am depressed and I ask myself these questions, I almost always start to change. I stop feeling sorry for myself and begin to take on the process of accountability. I begin to move and to feel confident. Soon I am energized and on my way. Yet the questions have wider potential.

Imagine what would happen if a leader came to understand the principles in these letters and then taught keys of profound possibility to all the people in his or her team, group, or organization. Imagine then if each person asked these questions regularly. Now take the image another step. Imagine what would happen if in that organization a new practice was adopted. No meeting could start without asking five questions: What result do we seek to create? Are we going to practice authentic commitment? Are we going to practice grounded vision? Are we going to practice adaptive confidence? Are we going to practice tough love? Suppose

The Integrated Wholonics Virtues.

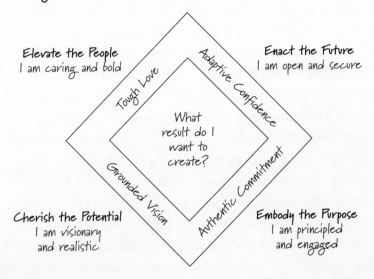

that no meeting could end without asking the same questions in review. Over time what would happen to such an organization?

First, when there was conflict, people would distort the values. Someone who thought the group was being too conservative might say, "We are not practicing our vision." Someone else might respond, "It is grounded vision, not just vision, and we need to be practical." Such an exchange would be especially valuable. Why? The conflict would make clear the validity of both positions and would create a necessity to explore for the meaning of grounded vision. It would cause the group to search for itself outside the comfort zone. This process would also do something else. It would be a source of constant instruction for the individual members of the organization. Over time they would learn to use Wholonics reasoning. They would have tools for making profound contact and profound contribution.

Let me end with a note about leadership. Leadership is not about learning techniques. It is about the clarification of purpose and the courageous pursuit of that purpose. When we lead in that way, we live in the Wholonics being state. This may sound like high philosophy. Yet there is empirical evidence for at least part of my claim. In a study of transformational leadership by Gibbons, the researcher looked into the developmental life experiences of transformational leaders. The researcher first identified transformational leaders and then did retrospective interviews with those leaders. One of the conclusions was that transformational leaders tended to have parents who provided them with difficult challenges but also supported them in their efforts if they failed or if they succeeded. In our words, the parents practiced tough love. I suspect that if future researchers look, they will find that those parents tended also to practice authentic commitment, grounded vision, and adaptive confidence. Given that likelihood, and given challenge to be a model, my favorite passage from your last letter was this:

> It's funny, but I'm not discouraged by the number of things I need to work on. The reason for this is that there are many things that any single person needs to work on. When you indicate your weaknesses, I find that helpful to think about. It gives me some hope. In most people's minds, Bob Quinn is nearly perfect. Yet they have no idea the number of things that you feel you need to work on. They would never even suggest that you may be in the precontemplation stage on some things. To them the idea would be preposterous. But when we truly look at ourselves, we can find all kinds of things that are wrong with us. We all practice foolish freedom.

If the leader's role is to help enlarge the capacity for moving up the great life spiral, the parent's role and the child's role are the same. We need to inspire each other toward more and more responsible freedom. I am glad that you can see me clearly enough to write a paragraph like the one you wrote. I hope our dialogues are so increasingly transparent that we can always find courage in each other's struggles.

You and I both know that life is hard. Like the history of Istanbul, our history is not a linear line pointing straight upward. You and I keep moving forward and backward as we keep moving up. Like the differentiated cultures that met in Istanbul, you and I can bounce off each other, or we can interpenetrate and enlarge each other. Life is not about survival. It is about survival and contribution. As you and I exercise the courage to grow, we increase the likelihood of living in possibility and contributing to the systems around us. We become transformational, driven by the good of the system and by moral principle. In that state, we can more clearly see that the purpose of life is to attract others to the great upward spiral. As we do that, we get glimpses as to where the great evolutionary spiral is taking us.

Love,

Dad

Ascend the Upward Spiral

Dear Garrett,

Thanks for your letter. It was my favorite. I liked it because you seem to be making so much progress. As you say, you are becoming happier. I was struck by the reasons you gave for being happier. Your appointments with your psychologist have been "productive," and you are understanding a lot more about yourself and why things are happening in your life. It is thrilling to realize that a few months ago you were resisting the notion of seeing a professional, and now you have a relationship with a psychologist that you really value.

I also liked your analysis of the impact of losing in the state tournament:

> *I didn't understand how something I had worked so hard for could be taken from me like that. It was a huge blow for me to take. It caused me to begin my "slow death." Subconsciously I decided that I wouldn't put any effort into anything because it would end up being a waste of my time. This is of course not true, but I truly believed it. So for this past year I have done absolutely nothing. I haven't come out of my comfort zone, I haven't made any attempt to get out of the process of entropy, and most of all, I haven't allowed myself to love anything because I knew that it would just lead to pain.*

This is a description of every human life. We all experience pain that we cannot understand. We then withdraw and begin to slowly die. We stop working, we stop growing, and we stop loving. Usually the choice of slow death requires that we manufacture some self-deception. You write, "This is of course not true, but I truly believed it." To avoid the pains of reality, we all spend a lot of time living in lies.

In the course of the past months you have traveled through the stages of change and have obtained a great payoff. You have now come to a great understanding:

> *I can't just stay in my comfort zone anymore, or else I might end up stuck in it forever. If I were reading this two months ago, I would have laughed and said, "Isn't that a little dramatic?" Well, yes, it probably is, but it's also true. I've seen it and felt it firsthand, and I hope I never do again.*

I too hope you never do again. Unfortunately, like the rest of us, you may again find yourself moving downward. Remember the story James Prochaska tells about getting depressed after high school and then having it happen again later. It took him several iterations to learn the things he needed to learn to effectively live his life. All of us keep choosing slow death because we keep losing the courage to face the realities in our lives. Living meaningfully requires that we constantly clarify our purpose and make courageous fundamental decisions. When we do, both our consciousness and our vision expand.

Yesterday I watched a group expand its vision. I was working with a company that was recently spun off from very large company. In the morning I had the participants do an organizational self-analysis. They were clear that their survival was predicated on better innovation, risk, and growth. Yet all through the rest of the day, as I gently but consistently pulled them toward more honesty and authenticity around the personal requirements of innovation, risk, and growth, they withdrew. They fought to stay in their comfort zones, to live by their egos. I kept at them, and by the end of the afternoon the resistance was gone and the room took on a tone of reverence. The dialogue became very intimate, very real, and full of greatness. Many of the participants were beginning to see how they could integrate who they were with what they do. That is always a critical moment in the onward journey. One older man walked up to me afterward and said, "This was the best day I have ever had in a classroom."

Why was he reacting positively? During the course of the day we found the courage to see reality more fully. As we exercised that courage, people began to see possibilities that they had not seen before. You have progressed this year, and you are now seeing things you could not see last September. You are much more full of possibility. Leadership is very much about seeing possibilities and helping others see them. Here is a story worth thinking about.

I recently attended a professional meeting in which my friend, Warren Bennis, made a presentation. Warren showed a video clip of an interview he did with the former president of a Quaker college. Because it was a Quaker institution, a core value of the college was nonviolence. In the middle of the interview the president talked of a particularly important moment in his tenure.

It was the height of the Vietnam War. Protests were frequent and often turned violent. The shooting of the students at Kent State had already occurred. Word came to him that a group of his students were going to hold a protest. They were going to take down the American flag and burn it. He also heard that members of his football team had gathered around the flagpole and were going to prevent the burning.

Imagine his feeling at that moment. Nonviolence is the core value, and it is about to be violated. He wants to preserve that value and does not want the conflict to take place. Such a conflict would split the college. What does one do in such a situation?

Most normal reactions would suggest taking control, perhaps calling in security and a large police backup. Yet all such alternatives have the likelihood of increasing the probability of conflict and violence. An entirely different perspective is to accept and withdraw. Just accept the reality that conflict happens. Stay out of it and let nature take its course. Then pick up the pieces. There are many arguments that could be made for that alternative.

What did he do? He walked out of his office and right up to the flagpole. What was his intended strategy? He had none! He did not know what to do. He felt helpless and vulnerable but knew that to be true to himself, he had to go to the flagpole. This is often the great moment, the essence of the leader's journey. It is the time when we must exercise faith and move forward in the face of un-certainty; it is the practice of adaptive confidence.

In the interview the president impresses the viewer as a strong-minded man. Yet as he gets to this moment in the story, he begins to weep. Why? He says that as he arrived on the tumultuous scene, he heard the voice of inspiration say to him, "Tell them to wash the flag."

He turned to the demonstrators and said, "Why don't you get a box of detergent and a bucket of water and wash the flag? Then when it is clean, run it back up the flagpole." Both the demonstra-tors and the football players found this to be an acceptable option. The flag was washed and put back up.

This is a moment that often occurs in transformational work. It is the moment when a leader articulates an image that tran-scends differences. The leader provides some form of atonement—"at-one-ment." In this case the image lifts the differentiated actors toward a more integrated and complex way of seeing and being. They are more whole or one.

By exercising the courage to walk into that difficult situation, the president was modeling authentic commitment. Such an ac-tion can be terrifying for most people because most of what we do comes from the ego and does not reflect authentic commitment. The president was willing to risk rejection and even physical harm.

He loved the community enough to put himself at the risk of being differentiated from it, even destroyed by it. Such love integrates what could not be integrated before.

Actually there is much integration going on in the story. Think for a moment about the image of washing the flag and putting it back up. The flag is a symbol of values such as freedom and democracy. The flag is also a symbol of our past sacrifices, of fathers, brothers, uncles, and friends dying for the values the flag represents. It is a symbol of our best collective self. Clearly it is worth defending. Yet in the Vietnam period, leaders of the same community were sending our people to die for reasons that were not so clear. They were engaged in a strategy that seemed to lack authentic commitment, causing our own commitment to wane. In people's minds, the flag can stand for the best of what we are or the worst. The protesters could see that something was wrong, and for them the flag became a symbol of hypocrisy, entropy, and evil. For them, it clearly deserved to be taken down and burned.

Washing suggests that we can cleanse what has been corrupted. Washing suggests that our past values, cleansed of our current hypocrisy, can create a desired future we can all embrace with authentic commitment. Washing represents the moment of interpenetration of two positive values. Washing redefines the two ends of the underlying polarity. Each becomes a positive. The positives are then integrated. The new construct suggests a stage of connection in which two positive poles become synergistic elements of a new state.

The story just told can be connected to the message of most spiritual traditions. In those traditions, we are the flag. Our task is to wash away hypocrisy, to integrate a past positive self and a future positive self. When we have such moments, we become aware of an alternative reality in which all things are connected, and this becomes a key turning point. To understand the power of such a moment, we must ask another question: In retelling the story, why did the president begin to cry?

Here is my best guess. He was fully extended, giving his best self, when he heard a voice. That voice or image came from outside his conscious mind. At that moment the inner and outer worlds merged. The image transformed everyone involved. The president, in a moment of extreme need, had an unexplainable resource come to his support. The experience produced feelings of insight, discovery, awe, peace, love, and oneness. In short, he could feel greatness, and that greatness was not coming *from him* but rather *through him*. Years later, simply telling the story still calls forth the same pattern of positive emotions.

I like the idea that when we increase our courage and exercise our faith, we increase our integrity, and greatness then flows through us. The claim makes me think about the scene in *The Empire Strikes Back* in which Yoda is teaching Luke Skywalker:

> *Size matters not. Look at me. Judge me not by my size, do you? Hm. Mmmm. And well you should not. For my ally is the Force. And a powerful ally it is. Life creates it, makes it grow. Its energy surrounds us and binds us. Luminous beings are we . . . not this crude matter. You must feel the Force around you. Here, hidden between you . . . me . . . the tree . . . the rock . . . everywhere! Yes, even between this land and that ship.*

I once heard an interview with one of the actors in the *Star Wars* movies. He said that he received more questions about the Force than any other single topic. He indicated that people are really interested in the idea of the Force. You may remember the scene in which Yoda explains that the Force is everywhere, that it surrounds and binds us. In relation to the quote from Yoda, one of my colleagues at the Michigan Business School, Tim Fort, and his associate James Noone, write: "One could substitute quotes similar to Yoda's from Buddhism, Hinduism, many yogis, many native religions and the Christian tradition, to name just a few religious sources. Indeed the connectedness of reality has philosophical support from Spinoza to Whitehead, as well as in the writings of many feminists and philosophers of science."

Experiencing support at the transformational moment, seeing the connectedness of reality, feeling the power that the college president felt and that Yoda described, is not always easy.

When you felt devastated by the loss in the state tournament, it sent you into a tailspin, and at that point nothing was easy. It took hard work to move forward and grow. It is when we exercise the faith to move forward that we tend to feel the connectedness I am talking about.

Over a lifetime, we have many failures and successes. When I reflect on mine, I realize that connectedness is very important to me. In my life statement you may remember the section I call my "Theological Core." It states some of my core beliefs. It was a late addition to my life statement. It came after a conversation in which I was asked to speak to a group of people who were committed to living spiritual lives. I asked them to articulate what they believed, not from reading or indoctrination, but from their direct experience with growth, enlightenment, and oneness. Specifically I asked them, "What do you know because God told you directly?"

Most had to stop and think about the question. Then they had to decide if they had the courage to share their answers. Slowly, first one and then another began to do so. They told of personal spiritual experiences and what they knew because of their experiences. Some were dramatic and some were simple, but all were compelling. In fact, I could not stop thinking about what they said. As a result, I went home and decided to write a statement that represented my theological core:

I experience myself as a being of spirit, light, truth, or intelligence engulfed in a body of physical matter. I experience a constant struggle between the pursuit of higher purpose and the enactment of selfish ends. In the midst of my life struggles, I experience a process called revelation. Revelation is not just insight or knowledge. Revelation is a process of discovery that changes my being state in a specific way.

When I experience revelation, I experience an increase in light, truth, intelligence, or spirit. It purifies, integrates, and enlarges me. My motives are elevated. My heart and mind become one, and I feel whole. I am enlarged in awareness and capacity. I become aware that light, truth, intelligence, or spirit is everywhere around me and that I am separated from these resources by darkness engendered by my fears. My capacity increases in that I become less shackled by my fears and move purposefully and confidently forward in the face of uncertainty.

In this process I take on a new or fresh view of the universe, of the world, and of myself. At the universal level, my sense of a supreme and benevolent intelligence increases. At the world level, my sense of scarcity is replaced by a sense of abundance. At the level of self, I become more internally driven and more other-focused. I clarify my purpose and increase in my yearning to help others. My grosser orientation is bridled, and I increase in virtues like gentleness, meekness, and love. As I radiate this purer love and act in patterns that enlarge others, I am further filled with light, truth, intelligence, or spirit. In this state I seem to attract others into new patterns of higher purpose, and the light in them burns more brightly. The intensified light in them further illuminates me. We become connected in the cocreation of light. In this process I feel that I am on a path toward a higher end.

I believe that my purpose is refinement of my gross self on life's great upward spiral.

   For these reasons, I yearn for revelation. I know the proba-bility of having revelation increases when I expose myself to faith-promoting stimuli and when I exercise self-mastery and experience victory over self. Faith-promoting stimuli include the past and present revelatory experiences of others and my own past revelatory experiences. When I read or listen to the revelatory experiences of others, I am more likely to take positive action. When I ponder my own past revela-tory experiences, I am even more likely to take positive action. When I search my present experiences for purposeful implications and revelatory indications, I am still more likely to take positive action. Cherishing revelation increases the probability of having revelation. In reflecting on past positive actions, I find the courage to move forward in faith, in re-flecting on that experience I further develop. As I so develop, I increase in light, truth, intelligence, or spirit, and I sense I am moving toward a transformation of profound importance.

I have spent the past three decades trying to help people and organizations change, and in the process I have come to learn a number of things about the spiritual nature of change and changing. For me there is an informal theology of change. Deep change always raises anxiety because the process and outcome are unpredictable. Deep change tends to be terrifying. To make deep change is to exercise faith and courage. It eventually results in dramatic increases in understanding and progress.

In my life statement I write, "I experience myself as a being of spirit, light, truth, or intelligence engulfed in a body of physical matter." This statement is a differentiation. I see myself as a physi-cal being and as a spiritual being. There is a struggle between my two orientations. The first leads me to entropy, and the second calls me to the work of change and the evolution to a higher level of consciousness and capacity. As I exercise discipline over myself, I come to the experience of revelation and an integration of the physical-spiritual differentiation.

I think of a remarkable story about connectedness. I once read a book on personality types by Riso and Hudson. In it was a surprising account told by one of the authors, Don Riso. His experience unfolded during a religious retreat. It was a physically grueling experience designed to bring out the deeper aspects of people. One afternoon there was an hour of free time, and most of the exhausted male participants went to their dorm room to take a nap. As most of the men were falling off to sleep, another man named Alan came in. Alan was angry about something and began to bang around in what seemed to be an intentional disturbance. Riso was starting to get angry about it. He then reports having an unusual experience:

> But shortly after Alan came crashing through the door, something amazing happened to me: I saw my negative reactions to him rising in my body like a train pulling into a station, and I did not get on the train. In a moment of simple clarity, I saw Alan with his anger and frustration—I saw his behavior for what it was without further elaboration—and I saw my anger "loading up" to let him have it—and I did not react to any of it.
>
> When I simply observed my reactions of anger and self-justification rather than acting on them, it was as if a veil were suddenly pulled from my eyes, and I opened up.
>
> Something that normally blocked my perception dissolved in an instant, and the world became completely alive. Alan was suddenly lovable, and the other guys were perfect in their

reactions, whatever they were. Just as astonishingly, as I turned my head and looked out the window, I saw that everything around me was flowing from within. The sunlight on the trees, the swaying of the leaves in the wind, the slight rattle of the panes of glass in the old window frame, were too beautiful for words. I was enthralled at how miraculous everything was. Absolutely everything was beautiful.

I was still in this state of amazed ecstasy when I joined the rest of the group for a late-afternoon meditation. As the meditation deepened, I opened my eyes and looked around the room—and fell into what I can only describe as an inner vision, the impression of which has stayed with me for years.

What I saw was that everyone there was a "being of light." I saw clearly that everyone is made of light—that we are like forms of light—but that a crust has formed over it. The crust is black and rubbery like tar and has obscured the inner light that is everyone's real, inner self. Some blotches of tar are very thick; other areas are thinner and more transparent. Those who have worked on themselves for longer have less tar and they radiate more of their inner light. Because of their personal history, others are covered with more tar and need a great deal of work to get free of it.

After about an hour the vision grew dim and eventually shut down. When the meditation was over, we had more work to do, and I rushed to take one of the most frequently avoided tasks, washing dishes in the steamy kitchen. But because the residue of ecstasy was still palpable, that chore, too, was a moment of bliss.

In reading this story, I am struck by a number of things. First of all, Riso reports moving out of his reactive stance. He had feelings of anger and self-justification but did not react. He chose not to react to his negative emotions. When we learn to choose, originate, and initiate, we become internally driven actors. We are no longer externally determined. We are free. We are creators. When Riso did not "get on the train," he chose to act rather than to react. He chose to be internally directed. This opened him up to see the world differently. He became open to new possibilities.

In my life statement I write, "I become aware that light, truth, intelligence, or spirit is everywhere around me and that I am separated from these resources by darkness engendered by my fears." In the story about Alan, Riso indicates that a veil fell from his eyes, his perception changed, he opened up, and he felt completely alive. I think this is what happens when we enter the extraordinary being state: we feel and see differently. Once Riso became more internally directed, he felt love for people despite their behaviors.

When we are creators and not reactors, we see people more deeply. No matter how bad their behavior, we see them with love. When we do this, it becomes more likely that our souls will touch. We make profound contact and cocreate increased light and truth. We call others forth to new and higher possibilities. This is the essence of wholonic leadership, calling people to higher levels of possibility.

Once in the extraordinary being state, Riso reports that all systems are flowing from within and are beautiful. He also suggests that everyone is a being of light:

Something that normally blocked my perception dissolved in an instant, and the world became completely alive. Alan was suddenly lovable, and the other guys were perfect in their re-actions, whatever they were. Just as astonishingly, as I turned my head and looked out the window, I saw that everything around me was flowing from within. The sunlight on the trees, the swaying of the leaves in the wind, the slight rattle of the panes of glass in the old window frame, were too beautiful for words. I was enthralled at how miraculous everything was. Absolutely everything was beautiful.

I particularly note these phrases: "the world became completely alive," "I saw everything was flowing from within," and "everything was beautiful." These observations suggest that there is life, light, or pure energy in all things, that everything is alive. This is the claim of Yoda and of most of the world's religions and of many philosophers. Yet if this is true, why is it so hard to see? The answer may also be embedded in the story. Riso points out that there is a dark crust over the light in people and the crust or black substance obscures the light. He tells us that people who have worked on themselves have a thinner crust and thus radiate more of their inner light, while some people, because of what has happened to them, have a thicker crust and need to do much work to become free of it.

I often have the feeling that we all ebb and flow in terms of light and darkness. I believe this is true about myself. There are times when I am radiant. I feel enthusiastic and have much to offer. There are times when I am depressed and have little to offer. My crust gets thicker. Given your experiences of the past year, Garrett, I think you can appreciate this. In comparison to last year, you have a much thinner crust; you are much more radiant. Last year you saw other people in a pretty negative light. Now you seem to see people in a much more positive light.

I have become committed to personal transparency, or trying to live with a very thin crust. I fail often, but I keep trying. In the end I think that this is the challenge awaiting anyone who wishes to be an agent of change. Helping others change requires that I transcend my ego, that I integrate my inner being and my outer circumstances. I come back again and again to the story about Shauri. On the way home from the airport, she hated her friend Matt and was destroying herself by choosing to live in negative emotion. After she clarified her purpose, her courage increased, and she saw a much brighter world. She then developed an increased love for people, even the friend who was at the center of her problems.

Because of our fears and our defense mechanisms, we avoid and distort reality. We choose to live in a reactive world of scarcity and threat. We work to acquire things, accumulate power, and exercise control without love. As a result, our crust grows thicker and everything seems to get darker. Soon we have what we most fear: disconnection, separation, and loneliness. In this state we know that Yoda is wrong. The last thing we would ever do, like the college president, is walk into an angry crowd with no strategy or tools of protection and control. We have no reason to do such a thing.

In my life statement I wrote, "In this process I take on a new or fresh view of the universe, of the world, and of myself." Life has taught me that when I exercise the discipline to do spiritual work, I grow. The keys to such growth are conscience and consciousness. The conscience is my sense of right and wrong, my sense of principles, scruples, ethics. When I allow it to operate, it drives me toward discipline, service, connection, purpose, and sacrifice. Yet I do not get there on a linear path. If I fail but keep going, I learn. I move up the learning spiral. As I do so, consciousness or awareness is further enlarged. I see things I did not previously see or know. Into my conscious mind comes a fresh view of reality, a fresh view of the universe, of the world, and of myself.

The word *repentance* has been used in ways that have caused it to take on a very dark overtone. We tend to distance ourselves from the word. Yet the word also conveys a sense of continually changing, growing, and increasing in consciousness of reality. Having a fresh view of reality means a new and recent vision, not one that is old and stale. There is a big difference between bread that is old and bread that is freshly baked. Our responsibility is to be fresh, to become new every day. Our responsibility is to thin the crust or reduce the ego barrier between our inner and outer worlds, to be a whole person.

The problem is that gaining fresh consciousness is work. I often take the easy path. I hold on to my old interpretations of reality and refuse to embrace the reality that is now emerging. I then feel guilt, shame, and other negative emotions. At this moment I have a really important choice: I can reconstruct myself or I can reconstruct God.

Normally I choose to reconstruct God. I create a new God after my own deficient or split image. This new God tends to exercise power without love and leads me into increased darkness. The challenge is to instead reconstruct myself, to take down the ego boundary, to exercise the faith to follow my conscience, to face my fears, to risk loss. In so doing, I become a new person with a fresh view of God, of the world, and of myself. I discover connected reality. In reconstructing myself, instead of God, I find the true and living God, and I am invited to advance on the great spiral.

There is a feedback loop that works as I advance. As I follow conscience, I increase consciousness. As I increase consciousness, my conscience becomes still more sensitive and more demanding. It calls on me to do still more. Again I have a choice: I can do the work of spiritual growth or distort the nature of emergent reality. If I do the former, I continue to grow; if I do the latter, I stop growing. The process goes on and on. How I work with the process and what state I am in depend on the choices I make.

When we choose to move forward, we are more open to "revelation." *Revelation* means "uncovering," but uncovering what? Many would answer, uncovering God. The logic is that God uncovers Himself by giving us revelation. That may be backward.

The Hebrew tradition begins with the story of Adam and Eve who lived in the Garden of Eden in a state of innocence and purity. They walked with God. They eventually faced a temptation. By partaking of the fruit of the forbidden tree, they could come to know good (positive) from evil (negative). To do so they would have to eat from the tree of knowledge. The choice to do so would allow them to become increasingly sophisticated (positive) in the discerning of good and evil, but it would cost them their innocence or purity and therefore their opportunity to be with God (positive). They were cast out of His presence. The very next thing that happens is that Adam and Eve become aware of their nakedness. They make aprons or clothes to cover their nakedness. When they then hear the voice of God in the garden, they hide from Him. When God calls, Adam is hiding. Adam tells God that he was hiding because of his nakedness.

I think that is what I often do. I hide from God. My conscience is calling me forth to engage in the work of growth, to become more conscious or sophisticated about reality (positive) and more pure or innocent (positive). My conscience is thus calling on me to transcend the split that occurred in the Garden of Eden by integrating positive opposites, sophistication and knowledge with innocence and purity. It is calling on me to live with authentic commitment, to be wholonic. I am often lazy and unwilling to do the work involved. I therefore feel shame and guilt and wrap myself in the aprons of my own rationalizations. In the process I also feel the need to hide my nakedness, my core self, from God and from others. Again I wrap myself in aprons of power, control, and status. I do a lot of posturing, a lot of pretending. I do not want anyone to see the real me, the naked me, the me that is so deficient and shameful. My crust or ego boundary thickens.

Remember that *revelation* means "uncovering" and that
the question is "Uncover what?" I suggest that revelation is not the
process of God uncovering Himself. It is the process of us uncovering ourselves. We find God as we take off our aprons of
rationalization. When we have the faith and courage to confront
truth and exercise victory over self, we commune with God. We
bring together our conscience and our consciousness. When
we exercise the faith and courage to uncover the blanket of darkness beneath which we hide, we find God. Why? Because at our
core we are not evil; we are inherently good.

At our core is the conscience, light, truth, or energy that is
God. The conscience is designed to help us evolve upward toward
the full flourishing of our best self. That progress is best stopped
by fear and rationalization. Under those coverings, or black
crusts, are light and truth and power. When we transcend the ego
boundary, conscience and the consciousness interpenetrate and
spiral upward. They are both increased in that the consciousness
expands and the conscience become a more sensitive and demanding force. We are more driven to be better and more aware of how
to be better.

Most transformational change agents understand this. I find
it most interesting that Nelson Mandela, the man who transformed South Africa, would include the following reading, from
the work of Marianne Williamson, in one of his early addresses:

> *Our deepest fear is not that we are inadequate. Our deepest
> fear is that we are powerful beyond measure. It is our light,
> not our darkness, that most frightens us. We ask ourselves,
> Who am I to be brilliant, gorgeous, talented, fabulous?
> Actually, who are you not to be? You are a child of God.
> Your playing small doesn't serve the world. There is nothing
> enlightened about shrinking so that other people won't feel*

insecure around you. We are all meant to shine, as children do. We were born to make manifest the glory of God that is within us. It's not just in some of us; it is in everyone. And as we let our own light shine, we unconsciously give other people permission to do the same. As we're liberated from our own fear, our presence automatically liberates others.

This statement suggests that we really are children of God and that we are born to "manifest the glory of God that is within us." When we manifest it, others are elevated. Perhaps one of the clearest advocates of this position is Scott Peck. He has spent his life trying to help people transform themselves. As a psychiatrist, he originally had a great mistrust of spiritual principles but eventually came to integrate them with his understanding of psychiatry. He then wrote one of the best-selling books of all time, *The Road Less Traveled.*

In the book he argues that the progress of the humankind is dependent on each person's ability to do spiritual work, to bring truth from the unconscious to the conscious level. He identifies three levels: the conscious self, the unconscious self, and the collective consciousness, which is outside of us. He claims that the collective conscious is God or Yoda's Force, or connected reality. The unconscious is the connection between God and our conscious mind. According to him, the entire purpose of life is spiritual growth. But why does God want us to grow? Peck provides a radical answer:

For no matter how much we may like to pussyfoot around it, all of us who postulate a loving God and really think about it eventually come to a single terrifying idea: God wants us to become Himself (or Herself or Itself). We are growing toward Godhood. God is the goal of evolution. It is God who is the

source of the evolutionary force and God who is the destina-
tion. This is what we mean when we say that He is Alpha
and Omega, the beginning and the end.

   When I said that this is a terrifying idea, I was speaking
mildly. It is a very old idea, but by the millions, we run from
it in sheer panic. For no idea ever came to the mind of man
which places upon us such a burden. It is the single most
demanding idea in the history of mankind. Not because it is
difficult to conceive; to the contrary, it is the essence of sim-
plicity. But because if we believe it, it then demands from us
all that we can possibly give, all that we have. It is one thing
to believe in a nice old God who will take care of us from a
lofty position of power which we ourselves could never begin
to attain. It is quite another to believe in a God who has it
in mind for us precisely that we should attain His position,
His power, His wisdom, His identity. Were we to believe it
possible for man to become God, this belief by its very nature
would place upon us an obligation to attempt to attain the
possible.

Peck goes on to argue that the goal of spiritual growth is the
attainment of godhood by the conscious self. It is not the goal for
the conscious to merge with the unconscious to live in some kind
of primitive, Eden-like innocence. It is not to be like an egoless
baby. It is to be simultaneously innocent or pure (positive) and
sophisticated or conscious (positive); it is to know with God, to
have the consciousness of God. Using my own language, we know
God when we live in authentic commitment. Living in authentic
commitment brings us to a point of ultimate transformation.

   I indicated that Peck's position is radical. It might more
accurately be called blasphemous. Why? The statement makes
humans equal to God. In most religious traditions there is an

assumed differentiation between God and humans. God is inherently good (positive), and humans and their physical bodies are inherently bad or evil (negative). For humans to claim equality with God is blasphemous. Some say it is the reason that Adam and Eve were banished from Eden!

I said earlier that when I am in the dark valley, I often choose to reconstruct God. When I do, I reconstruct Him in my own deficient and split image. That God and I are unconnected. He is good and I am bad. We just agree to leave each other alone. The God I create thus asks little of me in terms of working to overcome the entropy in my life. In fact this God colludes with me in my own destruction. This God becomes the nice old God that Peck describes.

If, in the valley I reconstruct myself, I encounter a very different God. Work takes me to the edge of my capacity, and there I must do the additional work of surrender. I allow my ego boundary to collapse as I do the excruciating work of stepping forward in faith (positive). As I do so, I experience grace (positive). As the experience and outcome interpenetrate, I am propelled up the spiral. As my consciousness increases, I find that I am inherently good and filled with love. I also find a God who is inherently good and filled with love. He wants to interact with me. He wants to become one with me. He practices authentic commitment and works for the good of our relationship. He radiates a grounded vision in which I begin to see my own potential. He radiates adaptive confidence that increases my faith. He practices tough love, inspiring progress on the spiral according to the exercise of my own responsible freedom.

In coming to know this God, I come to another radical insight: God is not a monopoly. Monopoly means having exclusive possession or control of something. Over time, monopolies tend to collapse. Monopolies usually result in the exercise of power without love. Think of the Saturday morning cartoons. The evil character is often some person who wants to gain control over the world for his or her own glory and power. This is the antithesis of God. God is not a monopoly. Yet many representations of God suggest that God is omnipotent and that in the celestial realm all things bow before God and give him glory forever and ever. So it sounds as if God has exclusive control of the resources in the universe. If he does, then why doesn't God collapse in on Himself?

The answer is that God is an integration of power (positive) and love (positive). The only way to expand in power and love is to continually grow. God grows in glory or light. Peck argues that when you or I become God, God then has a new life form. We become another manifestation of God, and light is increased in the universe. Possibility is enlarged. If God must grow, then God is dependent on us just as we are dependent on Him. He needs us to choose to move up the spiral. He needs us to grow because He is love and love cannot expand unless all parties in the relationship are benefiting. If we grow, He can grow. His light can radiate through us and further illuminate the universe. Light is intensified as life is expanded.

Here our tradition has relevance. The transformational core of Mormonism is found in a single statement: "As man is, God once was. As God is, man may become." From that starting point, Mormonism argues that God is Alpha, the spiritual light within (positive), and Omega, the perfected and resurrected physical man (positive), fused in love with a perfected father (positive male) and perfected mother (positive female). The purpose of life, then, is transformation of self, community, and the universe. As Peck suggests, a position such as this calls for enormous accountability and discipline. Such accountability and discipline tends to elevate and enlighten. It drives spiritual growth in the process of progression.

As we do the spiritual work of the upward spiral, we learn and internalize principles of truth. The discipline elevates us by increasing the light and power within us. We move forward and attract others to move with us. Through the internalization of higher and higher principles, or increased conscience and consciousness, we become one with God. The challenge, then, is not to escape the physical body. The challenge is to transform the body by integrating the physical (positive) and the spiritual (positive).

God is not a monopoly. Neither are we humans a monopoly. When we begin to act as if we are a monopoly, we become arrogant and controlling. Eventually we collapse. We and God are connected and inseparable. We need each other so as to cocreate and to increase in consciousness, to give meaning and life to each other and to the universe. Our task is the transformation of self and of community.

When we act, we act with motive, intention, or purpose. Our motive or intent matters a great deal because it helps determine the quality of our experience. If we do something without authentic commitment, we do it for external reasons, and there is no love in the act. Our body is involved, but we are not really present. At that moment we are exercising agency (positive) without love (negative). We are not exercising adaptive confidence and hence not growing up the spiral. We are owned by entropy. We have prostituted our possibility.

Most of us tend to see a sexual prostitute as a person engaged in dark behavior. We do not stop to think about why; we just know it is undesirable or evil. Why is it a dark pattern? A prostitute sells his or her body and engages in an act of physical intimacy (positive) with spiritual disconnection (negative). It is an act of agency or power without love or authentic commitment. The intimate act has the potential for concluding in one of the highest forms of interpenetration and transformation, the creation of a new life form. Yet the unstable relationship tends not to have the potential to support the life form. The act of prostitution is split at the outset. The actors are in a transactional relationship, simply using each other.

When we speak of prostitution, we often do so with great disdain. We thus distance ourselves from the evil therein. Yet with this distancing we judge ourselves by failing to see ourselves. There is hardly a moment that we are not guilty of similar acts. We all live in entropy all of the time. It is only when we do the work of spiritual growth, when we remove the ego barrier, that we reduce the positive-negative splits in our lives and act at the level of potential that results in profound contact and contribution.

It is important to know our own intention or motives at any given moment. It requires that we pay attention to our conscience. Our conscience tells us if we are in entropy. Yet the conscience is easily dulled by our rationalizations. Often as the ego boundary or crust grows thick, we can detect only the weakest of signals.

Yet the more we live by conscience, the better we can detect the signals it sends. When we make progress, all our unconscious resources become available to us because the conscious mind and the unconscious become one. We recognize that we are in the state of more authentic commitment. We then have greater trust and love for ourselves. We are less fearful of moving forward in the process of change. We increase in adaptive confidence. We develop grounded vision and we practice tough love. We are also more sensitive to spiritual things.

Spirituality is the state we enter when we become aware of the fact that we have transcended self. It is the state we enter when our crust grows thin. It is not entirely an internal affair. In the extraordinary being state we become like Yoda or Don Riso or many of the prophets: we can see things around us that we could not see before. We become more open to the light or truth or intelligence that permeates all matter. We discover that that form of purer matter is the power through which God works. Since we have increased in that light, we are closer to God, more able to understand the nature of God. As this process intensifies over time, we become aware of our relationship to God and of where the great spiral came from and where it is going.

It is most difficult to grow without a good community of practice. From the Buddhist tradition comes the work of Thich Nhat Hanh, a monk. In reflecting on the spiritual nature of humankind, he writes, "Transformational practice relies on the self, but a community and a teacher are also necessary." When he uses the word *community,* he means a place in which we find the discipline and the support for spiritual growth, a place where others are also trying to grow spiritually. I think of it as a place where we can cocreate the courage to be more spiritually naked. In my life statement I specify the need to share spiritual intimacies with others and to draw from theirs. Many communities do not facilitate such cocreation.

In discussing the concept of community Hanh notes that not all communities of practice are equally vital. There is considerable variation in the strength of communities. He offers an interesting insight:

> Any community of practice is better than a non-community of practice. Without a community of practice, you will be lost. To have a good community of practice, the members must live in a way that helps them generate more understanding and more love. If a community of practice is having difficulties, the way to transform it is to begin by transforming yourself, to go back to your island of self and become more refreshed and more understanding.

This is a beautiful but difficult concept. It is not natural to believe that the community about which we complain can be transformed by our transforming ourselves. It requires spiritual maturity to engage such a vision. It also recognizes that our light is cocreated. It is in the interaction between us and our community that light is generated. Because it is cocreated, we have the capacity to elevate our community. If we do increased spiritual work, if we increase in our own light, our light will change the community from which we seek support. If we give more light to the network of relationships in which we operate, we will get more light from them because there will be more light available. This happens as we search the self, remove the ego barrier, or make our crust thinner.

To search is to look for, seek, hunt, investigate, explore. Self can refer to the personality, character, identity, or basic nature. The self is who we are, our way of being. To search the self means that we explore or seek to know our very core or essence. It is asking the question, "Who am I?" In pondering this issue, I came across an interesting professional paper that discussed the nature of the self. Consider the following:

> Newtonian physicists were startled to discover that at the core of the atom, at the center of matter there is . . . nothing, no thing, pure energy. When they reached into the most fundamental building block of nature they found a pregnant void—stable patterns of probability striving to connect with other patterns of probability. This discovery revolutionized the physical sciences, initiating the quantum era.
>
> By the same token, we are startled to discover that at the core of the person, at the center of selfhood there is . . . nothing, pure energy. When we reach into the most fundamental basis of our being, we find a pregnant void, a web of relationships. When somebody asks us to talk about ourselves, we talk about family, work, academic background, sports

*affiliations, etc. In all this talk, where is our "self"? The
answer is nowhere, because the self is not a thing, but as
Jerome Bruner says, "a point of view that unifies the flow of
experience into a coherent narrative"—a narrative striving
to connect with other narratives and become richer.*

Now suppose that at our core we are nothing, no thing.
What if all matter is permeated by pure energy or light in search
of possibility? What if Yoda was right all along? What if at our core
there is only light, pure energy, spirit, or intelligence attempting to
connect to other forms of pure energy in ways that makes that
energy richer?

As God moves forward in His work, which is moving us
forward in purification and enlightenment, He intensifies His own
light, glory, or power. In the process we establish richer and purer
relationships with other people and with God. Our narrative and
their narratives become intertwined. The self is energized in
mutually enhancing relationships. It exists in a state of pure love,
which Saint Paul called charity. Through obedience and faith, we
become increasingly full of charity, full of intelligence, light, truth,
spirit, and godliness.

As we adhere to conscience and increase in consciousness,
we come to embody virtue. We become long-suffering, gentle,
meek, full of love, and enlightened by pure knowledge. These
characteristics of spirit, light, truth, or intelligence become
internalized and embodied in us. These godly characteristics then
become attractors that call forth the no-thingness or spirit, light,
and truth of others. Such relationships become a "coherent and
unified flow of experience," and everyone in the relationship
becomes richer in spirit, light, truth, and intelligence.

So what does it mean to find the self? To find the self is
to experience increased consciousness, increased capacity,

increased concern, and an enriched relationship with God and His offspring. Our own narratives and their narratives are intertwined so as to become one. Differences are integrated and transformed into one great whole or "at-one-ment." Our narrative and God's narrative are connected; they become an integrated system of meaning. We are animated by charity. We emanate power and love. We transform community. We live in oneness with others because we are one.

When we become more transparent, when we share what is most intimate, what we know by revelation, what shines most brightly within us, and what we feel most strongly about, we expose others to our light. Our stories of courage and spiritual growth increase their faith and courage. I am sure it took courage for the president of the college to tell the story of flag washing. I am sure it took courage for Don Riso to decide to share his story in his book. It has taken courage for me to share some of these thoughts with you and others. It has taken particular courage for you to share your story.

I must return to a sentence in Riso's story: "Alan was suddenly lovable, and the other guys were perfect in their reactions, whatever they were." How can people be perfect in their reactions no matter what those reactions are? It is because when we enter the extraordinary being state, we tend not to judge but to love. We do this because we see the best self in others, even if they cannot. We also realize that they are someplace on the great upward spiral, moving forward or backward as they learn their way toward increased light and life. Their story and our story are one.

That is how it is with you and me. You and I are both on the great upward spiral. Your story and my story are one. You and I are flags that need washing. You and I are positive oppositions becoming more fully integrated in love. As I close this last letter, I am reminded of a poem I wrote about you when you were nine years old:

GARRETT

Yesterday I watched you walking
In the sun.
Your nine-year-old body
Was like that of a great golden god.

It seems an appropriate vessel
For the integration
Of such a gentle heart
And relentless mind.

You carry light
You always have.
It penetrates my soul
And fills me
And makes me love you.

God is not a monopoly. You and I are not monopolies. You and I are in the same relationship with each other that each person is with God. To me you have always been a source of light. You inspire and lift me. I therefore always want to be with you. You were meant to grow, to become a radiant source of light, to have impact, to lead change. To do so means that greatness, the grace of God, must come through you and fill you with humility. To facilitate your ascendance of the great spiral, I would gladly die. I am authentically committed to the relationship that encompasses us and makes us one. I yearn that we might be united forever in love.

Love,

Dad

Long-Term Life Vision

I will continuously strive to reach a more authentic, complex, and vital being state. I will strive to have purpose, exercise faith, engage reality, reduce my hypocrisy gaps, and live an empowered (inner-directed) and empowering (other-focused) life. Living in this state, I will seek to put potential into the systems that surround me and facilitate their growth toward increased complexity. I will remember that the key is not the outcome but the being state. I will live in the extraordinary being state and attract people to profound possibility on life's upward spiral.

Short-Term Life Vision

I am healthy, active, and happy. I have a loving and productive relationship with each family member. I strive to value and elevate people. I am with professional purpose. I am full of charity, and virtue garnishes my thoughts, so my relationships are meaningful.

Professional Life Mission

To understand and facilitate change so as to help people, groups, and organizations encounter increased power, meaning, and success. To leave a legacy that is reflected in a philosophy and school of profound possibility.

General "Best Self" Characteristics

In enacting my best self, I tend to be creative. I am enthusiastic about ideas and craft bold visions. I am an innovative builder who perseveres in the pursuit of the new. I do not waste energy thinking about missed opportunities or past failures, nor do I take on the negative energy of the insecure, nor do I worry about the critics. I do not waste energy in defensive routines. I stay centered and focused on what is possible and important.

I have frameworks that allow me to make sense of complex issues. I get to the essence. I can see disparate ideas and integrate them through "yes-and" thinking. So I make points others do not readily see. I tend to be inner-directed, so my message comes from an authentic level. I think deeply and speak with conviction. In doing so, I frame experiences in compelling and engaging ways. I paint visions and provide new ways for people to see. I use metaphors and stories to do this. I find the stories in everyday experiences, and people find it easy to understand them. The new images that follow help people to take action.

In helping others, I see the possibility for greatness in people. I calm them while I energize them. I help people identify their own core ideas, core emotions, and core values, and it has a catalytic effect on how they feel and think. They see new possibilities, and the excitement helps them find the courage to act. I give them my attention and energy, but I allow them to be in charge.

In exercising influence, I do not try to think others into action. I try to enroll them in new directions. I try not to sell but rather to invite people into my journeys. In pursuing the journey, I seek reality. This means seeking honest dialogue. I do not get defensive or reject others if they are uninterested or if they choose to focus elsewhere. I make it clear that the relationship is more important than a conflict, and honest dialogue will improve things. At such times, I surrender my ego and invite criticism.

As a teacher and interventionist, I do not seek to inform but to transform. I use dialogue to help people surface their ideas, and then I weave those ideas together with others until we create knowledge in real time. In doing so, I move them from the abstract to the concrete and from the objective to the intimate. I ignore symptoms and focus on the deep causes. I ask piercing questions. I help people and groups surface the darkest realities and the most painful conflicts. From these emergent tensions comes the energy for transformation. I liberate people from their fears and help them embrace new paths. In all of this I try to model the message of integrity, growth, and transformation.

High-Performance Profile

When I am at my best, I tend to enter a meaningful situation that has the potential for increased synergy and long-term impact. I do not intrude. I am invited in because of perceived competence and credibility. I am integrated with a caring associate who tends to logistics and execution. I seek to understand the implicit processes and structures that drive the system. I search for the single bold stroke that will transform the existing paradigm. As I do so, I tolerate ambiguity, explore the parts, and conceptualize the whole. These grounded observations allow me to communicate images with confidence and passion. People feel and see alternatives.

I seek to both relate in a loving relationship and to challenge with high standards; in other words, I seek to be empowered and empowering. In doing so, I facilitate the creation of an emergent community of empowered people. Toward the end of the experience, I yearn for new stimulation and seek to manage the transition and movement to a new adventure.

High-Performance Roles

I am at my best when I play one or more of the following strategic roles.

Explorer: I seek personal and collective enlightenment at the edge of chaos.
Point guard: I seek to make the aggregate more than the sum of its parts.
Interviewer: I listen for the underrepresented collective voice.
Visionary: I conceptualize the unspoken need.
Facilitator: I bring to the surface the truth that is too painful to be engaged.
Storyteller: I attract people to change by sharing images that enable.
Role model: I attract people to change by achieving and exposing an authentic self.
Leader: I attract people to change through being change.

Daily Life Strategy Checklist

To accomplish these things, I am exercising, controlling diet, evolving physically, studying, praying, closing integrity gaps, experiencing inspiration, tending to family, tending to others, saving mornings for creative demands, controlling commitments, focusing professionally, disciplining finances, and playing.

Self-Empowering Questions

What result do I want to create?
Am I practicing authentic commitment?
Am I practicing grounded vision?
Am I practicing adaptive confidence?
Am I practicing tough love?

Theological Core

I experience myself as a being of spirit, light, truth, or intelligence engulfed in a body of physical matter. I experience a constant struggle between the pursuit of higher purpose and the enactment of selfish ends. In the midst of my life struggles, I experience a process called revelation. Revelation is not just insight or knowledge. Revelation is a process of discovery that changes my being state in a specific way.

When I experience revelation, I experience an increase in light, truth, intelligence, or spirit. It purifies, integrates, and enlarges me. My motives are elevated. My heart and mind become one, and I feel whole. I am enlarged in awareness and capacity. I become aware that light, truth, intelligence, or spirit is everywhere around me and that I am separated from these resources by darkness engendered by my fears. My capacity increases in that I become less shackled by my fears and move purposefully and confidently forward in the face of uncertainty.

In this process I take on a new or fresh view of the universe, of the world, and of myself. At the universal level, my sense of a supreme and benevolent intelligence increases. At the world level, my sense of scarcity is replaced by a sense of abundance. At the level of self, I become more internally driven and more other-focused. I clarify my purpose and increase in my yearning to help others. My grosser orientation is bridled, and I increase in virtues like gentleness, meekness, and love. As I radiate this purer love and act in patterns that enlarge others, I am further filled with light, truth, intelligence, or spirit. In this state I seem to attract others into new patterns of higher purpose, and the light in them burns more brightly. The intensified light in them further illuminates me. We become connected in the cocreation of light. In this process I feel that I am on a path toward a higher end. I believe that my purpose is refinement of my gross self on life's great upward spiral.

For these reasons, I yearn for revelation. I know the probability of having revelation increases when I expose myself to faith-promoting stimuli and when I exercise self-mastery and experience victory over self. Faith-promoting stimuli include the past and present revelatory experiences of others and my own past revelatory experiences. When I read or listen to the revelatory experiences of others, I am more likely to take positive action. When I ponder my own past revelatory experiences, I am even more likely to take positive action. When I search my present experiences for purposeful implications and revelatory indications, I am still more likely to take positive action. Cherishing revelation increases the probability of having revelation. In reflecting on past positive actions, I find the courage to move forward in faith, in reflecting on that experience I further develop. As I so develop, I increase in light, truth, intelligence, or spirit, and I sense I am moving toward a transformation of profound importance.

References

Bass, B. M. *Transformational Leadership: Industry, Military and Educational Impact.* Mahwah, N.J.: Erlbaum, 1998.

Csikszentmihalyi, M. *Finding Flow: The Psychology of Engagement with Everyday Life.* New York: Basic Books, 1997.

Fletcher, J. L. *Patterns of High Performance: Discovering the Ways People Work Best.* San Francisco: Berrett-Koehler, 1993.

Fort, T. L., and Noone, J. J. "Banded Contracts, Mediating Institutions, and Corporate Governance: A Naturalist Analysis of Contractual Theories of the Firm." *Law and Contemporary Problems,* 1999, *62*(3), 163–213.

Fritz, R. *The Path of Least Resistance: Learning to Become the Creative Force in Your Own Life.* New York: Fawcett Columbine, 1989.

Gibbons, R. C. "Revisiting: The Question of Born Versus Made: Toward a Theory of Development of Transformational Leaders." Doctoral dissertation, Fielding Institute, Santa Barbara, Calif., 1986.

Hanh, T. N. *Living Buddha, Living Christ.* New York: Riverhead Books, 1995.

Heifetz, R. A. *Leadership Without Easy Answers.* Cambridge, Mass.: Belknap Press of Harvard University Press, 1994.

Kershner, I. (dir.). *The Empire Strikes Back.* Lucasfilm,1980.

Kofman, F., and Senge, P. M. "Communities of Commitment: The Heart of Learning Organizations." *Organizational Dynamics,* 1993, *22*(2), 5–23.

La Barre, P. "Do You Have the Will to Lead?" *Fast Company*, Mar. 2000, p. 222.

Needleman, J., and Appelbaum, D. *Real Philosophy: An Anthology of the Universal Search for Meaning.* New York: Penguin Books, 1990.

Peck, S. *The Road Less Traveled: A New Psychology of Love, Traditional Values, and Spiritual Growth.* New York: Simon & Schuster, 1978.

Pirsig, R. M. *Zen and the Art of Motorcycle Maintenance.* New York: Morrow, 1974.

Prochaska, J. O., Norcross, J. C., and DiClemente, C. C. *Changing for Good: A Revolutionary Six-Stage Program for Overcoming Bad Habits and Moving Your Life Positively Forward.* New York: Avon Books, 1994.

Quinn, R. E. *Deep Change: Discovering the Leader Within.* San Francisco: Jossey-Bass, 1996.

Quinn, R. E. *Change the World: How Ordinary People Can Accomplish Extraordinary Results.* San Francisco: Jossey-Bass, 2000.

Riley, P. *The Winner Within: A Life Plan for Team Players.* New York: Putnam, 1993.

Riso, D. R., and Hudson, R. *The Wisdom of the Enneagram: The Complete Psychological and Spiritual Growth for the Nine Personality Types.* New York: Bantam Books, 1999.

Rothenberg, A. *The Emerging Goddess: The Creative Process in Art, Science, and Other Fields.* Chicago: University of Chicago Press, 1979.

Torbert, W. R. *Managing the Corporate Dream: Restructuring for Long-Term Success.* Homewood, Ill.: Dow Jones/Irwin, 1987.

Vaillant, G. E. *Adaptation to Life: How the Best and the Brightest Came of Age.* Boston: Little, Brown, 1977.

Williamson, M. A. *Return to Love.* New York: HarperCollins, 1994.

Acknowledgments

We want to thank the many people who helped. Many colleagues read portions of the manuscript. Jim Emrich, Thom Nielson, Lynda St. Clair, and Stuart Youngblood were kind enough to read and give us comments on the entire draft. Hal Zina Bennett did a marvelous job as our developmental editor. Kathe Sweeney and Byron Schneider gave us the loving discipline that kept us moving. Pauline Farmer was indispensable in managing us. Thanks to each one of these marvelous human beings. We want to especially thank our family for putting up with us in the process of this endeavor. It is not easy trying to figure out how to grow up.

REQ
GTQ

The Authors

ROBERT E. QUINN holds the Margaret Elliott Tracy Collegiate Professorship of Organizational Behavior and Human Resource Management at the University of Michigan Business School. He designs and teaches courses in the M.B.A. program and at the Executive Education Center. Quinn is the author of a number of books. Among the most recent are *Change the World: How Ordinary People Can Accomplish Extraordinary Results* (Jossey-Bass, 2000) and *Deep Change: Discovering the Leader Within* (Jossey-Bass, 1996). He has published numerous academic papers and texts on organization, leadership, and change. He currently serves as the consulting editor of the University of Michigan Business School Management Series published by Jossey-Bass. He is a noted speaker and consultant.

GARRETT T. QUINN lives in Ann Arbor, Michigan. In high school he participated in a number of the school's leadership activities. He particularly enjoyed athletics. As a junior he was the shooting guard on the basketball team that won the state championship. In his senior year he was cocaptain of the team and was named an all-area selection. He spent one year in college and is now working in Ann Arbor as he prepares to return to college.